From Where I Sit

Also by
Merv Griffin
with
Peter Barsocchini

MERV
An Autobiography

From Where I Sit

MERV GRIFFIN'S BOOK OF PEOPLE

by Merv Griffin

with Peter Barsocchini

ARBOR HOUSE
New York

This book is for all those gifted people who have been brave and generous enough to sit across the microphone from me and share the stories of their lives

CONTENTS

7

8

Including Reminiscences of . . .

George Burns · Conrad Nagel · Vincent Price · John Lennon · Rita Hayworth · Harry Houdini · Gerald R. Ford · Winston Churchill · John Barrymore · Marlene Dietrich · Greta Garbo · Coco Chanel · Bob Hope · Elizabeth Taylor · Sophia Loren · David Brenner · Howard Teichman · Margaret Sullavan · Jed Harris · Roger Vadim · Tom Heggen · James Stewart · Marilyn Monroe · Don Murray · John F. Kennedy · Christiaan Barnard · Hugh Downs · Prince Rainier and the late Princess Grace · Marlon Brando · John Derek · Truman Capote · Louella Parsons · Hedda Hopper · Cole Porter · Mike Todd · Harry Cohn · Sam Goldwyn · Louis B. Mayer · David O. Selznick · Gary Cooper · James Cagney · Edward G. Robinson · John Garfield · Errol Flynn · Al Pacino · Bertrand Russell · George Lucas · Richard M. Nixon · Spiro Agnew · Lyndon Johnson · E. Howard Hunt · William F. Buckley, Jr. · Robert Haldeman · John Erlichman · Dwight Eisenhower · Robert Kennedy, Jr. · Arthur Schlesinger · Theodore White · William Manchester · Walter Cronkite · John Chancellor · Menachem Begin · Anwar Sadat · Fidel Castro · Alex Haley · Truman Capote · Norman Mailer · Gore Vidal · Irwin Shaw

PREFACE

On October 1, 1962, I walked out on stage for the first "Merv Griffin Show." Twenty years and five thousand shows later, I'm still walking out on stage each day for a new edition of "The Merv Griffin Show." During these twenty years I've interviewed entertainers and political leaders, and seers, criminals and Communists, geniuses and ghost hunters, writers and even a few wrongdoers. In short, a ceaseless stream of cultural and social history has flowed in front of me for two decades, and that's what this book is all about: people.

When talk shows are at their best, they provide a sampling of what's going on in the world, recounted face to face by the people who make their living in the public arenas, whether it's in movies like Jane Fonda, in the courtroom, like Watergate judge John J. Sirica or on television, like Barbara Walters and Dan Rather.

When these people are guests on my show they get a chance to talk about their lives and their work, reflect on it, sometimes even complain about it. On talk shows we see these special people in a different light from their regular milieu. And that is what I'm hoping this book will do.

From where I sit, the past twenty years have been an entertaining and informative journey, and I hope this book is that for you.

MY NEXT GUEST

BETTE DAVIS—On Tallulah Bankhead:
"I did many parts on the screen that Tallulah did on stage. So at a party one night, about two in the morning, we were still there and she was loaded. Most of the guests had left and we found ourselves standing in a corner. She scared me to death. She said, 'Hello. You know, you've played all the parts I've played, and I have played them so much better.' And I said, 'Miss Bankhead, I couldn't agree with you more.' "

*

JACK BENNY
Master of the Setup

LET ME TELL you a few things I've noticed over the years about comedians. Rule number one is don't expect your favorite funnyman to be a lot of laughs offstage; most of them aren't. They are too busy thinking about last night's show or an upcoming performance to be tossing off jokes at random. There are exceptions—Don Rickles and George Burns are simply funny *people*—but don't expect Rodney Dangerfield or Joan Rivers to be cracking jokes if you run into them in an airport; their humor requires a certain atmosphere and they stick to it. My second rule is that comedians are hypochondriacs. Mention to a comic that he looks pale and he starts reserving space at Forest Lawn.

I knew a comedy writer who for years was convinced he had a brain tumor, and presented himself to a parade of doctors who categorically pronounced him well, but what did a damn doctor know? Finally, comedians are nuts. It's the toughest job in show business to stand in front of an audience trying to make them laugh. It is maddening for a comic when one night his material gets screams, and the next night the same material draws a blank. This produces interesting eccentricities. One of my joke writers was capable of turning out material only thirty minutes before showtime, and then only when he could stand in the dressing room, light a cigar, turn the water faucets on full force and blast rock music through the walls. *That* made him concentrate on being funny.

The best way I can sum up how a comedian thinks is through the classic story about the Las Vegas comic who was doing two shows a night, opening for Tom Jones at Caesars Palace. One night after his show he went into the hotel bar for a nightcap, and was approached by a gorgeous blonde who wore a slinky silk dress.

"You were just wonderful tonight," she told him. "I went to see Tom Jones but you were even better. The way you made me laugh was just so *sexy.* In fact, I don't think I've ever been so turned on by a man in my life. It was just the best show I've ever seen, and you know what I'd like to do? I'd like to go up with you to your room, order some champagne and make love to you all night."

The comedian looked at her thoughtfully, then said, "Did you see the early show or the late show?"

*

DOROTHY LAMOUR:
"I think both Bing Crosby and Bob Hope had sex appeal, but everybody laughs when I tell them something that I really and truly mean: I have always thought, and don't you dare tell him I said so, that Bob Hope has a *great* deal of sex appeal."

*

Now, having said all this about comedians, I'd like to talk about one of the exceptions to most of my rules, Jack Benny. He didn't consider himself funny offstage, though many of us did; he was *not* a hypochondriac, nor was he crazy. In fact, Jack was just about the sweetest man I've ever known in show business. By the time I met him in 1949 he was already a major

star, but there didn't seem to be a speck of pretense or self-importance in the man.

We were in Houston, Texas, for a gala show at Glen McCarthy's Shamrock Hotel. The bill for the big show featured Jack, Dinah Shore, Phil Harris, Les Brown and his Band of All Stars and Freddy Martin and his orchestra, for which I was lead singer. Mr. McCarthy had brought in stars and dignitaries from all over the country for this event, and he was hosting an elegant, private dinner prior to the show. On my way to the dinner I passed the hotel coffee shop, and there alone at the counter sat Jack Benny. He was chatting pleasantly with a waitress, and enjoying a pastrami sandwich and a chocolate milk shake. I popped in and tapped him on the shoulder. "Jack, they're serving a ten-course gourmet meal upstairs for us, and you're eating a pastrami sandwich in the coffee shop?"

"And enjoying every minute of it," he said simply, "I really am. I'm happier right here."

That's the way he was, and that's the way he stayed. Even when he and Mary hosted large parties for their famous friends, Jack preferred to sit in the kitchen, fix a sandwich and chat with the help. He was comfortable that way. Fame didn't burden him.

"Let me tell you how famous I am," he said to me once. "I was a very bad student, I hated school, and yet now they have a beautiful high school in Winnetka, Illinois, named after me, Jack Benny Junior High School. Every now and then I go to visit; particularly at the end of their school year, I'll go and give out diplomas. Because it's a junior high, some of the kids are so young they don't even know who I am, even at *Jack Benny* Junior High School. I gave little lectures to the different classes, and at one class where they have such young kids, after I talked a while, I said we ought to have questions and answers. A little girl raised her hand and said,

'Mr. Benny, why did they name you after our school?' "

I always found Jack to be witty and bright offstage, but he didn't consider himself a naturally funny man. His friend George Burns disagreed—he thought Jack was hilarious all the time. When I told that to Jack he shook his head.

"No, he doesn't. George Burns does *not* think I'm funny. He's saying it just to be nice. George Burns thinks I'm *clever*; he thinks I'm funny *onstage*. I think if you ask George, Who is the best comedian, he'd say Jack Benny. But he means onstage, where I'm getting paid. But I'm not funny at a house party like he is. I'm not funny *any*place, except when I'm working and that's the only place I *try* to be funny. I don't know how to be funny at a house party.

"I want to tell you what kind of dirty tricks George Burns plays. I've been invited to half a dozen royal Command Performances, and after the performances all the artists stand in line in the foyer of the theater while the Royal Family comes through—you meet them and shake hands and talk. Just as the Queen was approaching me, George Burns whispered in my ear, 'If you laugh it will be *very* embarrassing.' Isn't that a dirty, lousy trick to play on somebody?

"Another time I was at a dinner party and Jeanette MacDonald was singing for a few friends after dinner. George Burns came over and said, 'If you laugh while she sings, it'll be *aw*ful.' Then he stood in back of me, and I *knew* he was standing there. You can imagine what happened to me."

Jack also told me about the time he was to play the Palladium in London. He invited George Burns to come for opening night. George said he couldn't make it, but Jack kept asking. No way in the world, George told him. So on opening night George flew all the way to London, got a seat in the middle of the front row, sat through the show, then left immediately for the airport and returned to America. Now, Jack

Benny went crazy telling everybody that he was *sure* he saw
George Burns sitting in the front row. Everyone looked at Jack
like he was nuts, because George was nowhere to be found in
the city.

I think the secret to Jack's success in making us all laugh was
the fact that he had mastered the "setup"; he knew how to
create the atmosphere for something funny to happen. I got
my first lesson in his method the night Jack was doing the show
at the hotel opening in Houston. After finishing his pastrami
sandwich and milk shake, Jack came backstage and looked for
me.

"What I'd like you to do is this," he said. "I'm going to do
a violin solo at a certain point in my show. After a couple of
minutes of music I want you to take these pennies"—he
handed me a pocketful—"and start tossing them out on the
stage one by one. Just stand in the wings and slowly toss them
out there."

I had no idea what he had in mind. When he was a couple
of minutes into his violin solo—which was, of course, dreadful
—I began lobbing the pennies out onto the bare stage. He kept
right on playing. After I tossed a few more, people in the
audience began throwing pennies. Jack started to take sidelong
glances at the accumulation of coins. And just as the audience
was beginning to rumble with laughter, he put down his violin,
and patiently began picking up the change, coin by coin, and
dropping them into his pocket. The laughter turned to howls,
and I stood in the wings and admired the master's complete
control of timing.

Years later I asked Jack about his formula for getting laughs.
He told me a story to make his point.

"I knew I was going to make a film of 'George Washington

Slept Here,' and the studio sent me to New York to see the play. The play was not as successful as the picture was to be, but there was a fellow in it called Percy Kilbride who was the funniest man I'd ever seen. I came back to Hollywood and said to Jack Warner, 'I'll make 'The Horn Blows at Midnight,' which was another picture he wanted me to do, but you must bring Percy Kilbride out here. He's the funniest man I've ever seen.'

"Jack said, 'We've got too many comedians under contract.'

"I said, 'I don't care. Why not have a new face? I want him in the picture.'

"So Warner thought he'd trick me by saying, 'Well, Jack, if he's *that* funny, he'll steal your picture.'

"And I said, 'You're damn right he will, and *some*body better steal it, because I'm not going to steal it.' So that's how I got Percy Kilbride out here, and he *did* steal the picture. I don't care *who* steals it, as long as it was my show. Don't forget that on my television show, and before that radio, Rochester stole it, Phil Harris stole it, Dennis Day stole it, Mary stole it, everybody stole it . . . but it was *my* show. I've had people come up to me and say, 'You know, Jack, Rochester stole your show last night.' And I'd answer, 'You bet he did, and he better keep stealing it or he won't be with me, because that's what I want.' I want everybody to steal it. I've had half-hour shows where *I* haven't had one laugh, but it doesn't make any difference. It really doesn't make any difference *who* gets the laugh. This I've learned all my life in show business. As long as it is *my* show. If it's somebody else's show, then *I* want to get the laugh."

And those laughs on the Benny show were no accident. I watched them rehearse on many occasions, and often the set-ups were elaborate and tedious, but Jack patiently rehearsed until he was happy with all the elements; no temper tantrums, no scenes, just patient work until the atmosphere was right. That kind of humor takes a keen observer's eye, a feeling for detail, and Jack certainly had it.

Once when he was backstage for a guest appearance on my show, he stood in the wings and watched me for a few moments before the theme music started for my entrance. In those days I used to run out on stage on cue, pumped up for the performance. That night Jack followed me out, and when the applause subsided, he said, "Why do you *run* out on stage like that? You get all excited backstage, then you run out. You've got *ninety* minutes, Merv, what's the rush?"

The audience was laughing at Jack's simple observation. And I just stared at him for a while. I'd been running out on stage for ten years, never giving it a second thought; it was an unconscious habit. But once Jack pointed it out to me, I could never do it again, and I haven't since that night.

Most people think of Jack as a great television and radio star, but one afternoon I got him talking about his career in movies, and was surprised to learn that he'd made twenty-two of them, most of which were hits. "In those days," he told me, "if you spent a million dollars on a picture it was a lot of money; now you *have* to spend twenty or twenty-five million. In those days it didn't cost much, and because I was big in radio, my pictures really made quite a bit of money. Right back," he said, pausing and raising his eyebrows, "to 1928."

His movie career began with "The Hollywood Revue of 1928" at MGM. "That's the first time a picture was made of a revue where it was like a vaudeville show. Every star at MGM, except Greta Garbo and Lon Chaney, were in the picture, and I was master of ceremonies and had to introduce each one of them. In 'The Hollywood Revue' was the most embarrassing thing that ever happened to me in a picture.

"I got the job when I was playing the Orpheum Theater in Los Angeles. In fact, that's where I met Mary, my wife. She was working across the street in the May Company, selling ladies' hosiery. I saw Mary and liked her, and I thought that sometime I'd ask her to marry me, and I did. I used to walk in there all the time and ask her where the men's room was— that's how we got acquainted. Anyway, when you are master of ceremonies, you should have a good vocabulary. I was supposed to. Now, in this picture was Conrad Nagle, who was also a big star, and I was supposed to introduce him in this way: 'And now, ladies and gentlemen, we have Conrad Nagle, a name to conjure with.' And the director came over to me and said, 'We don't want you to use that word correctly, we want you to say, "Conrad Nagle, a name to con*jure* with."'

"But that's the wrong pronunciation," I protested. "It would look awful if I said 'a name to con*jure* with.'"

" 'Listen,' the director said, 'what we are doing is writing a comedy scene about the word *con*jure or con*jure*. Your line sets it up.'

"So I thought, well, all right, as long as they rectify it. I just didn't want to make a silly mistake like that in my first picture. Now, as you know, they don't shoot movies in sequence. They are liable to shoot the first scene last; you never know what's going to happen. I walked out and said 'Ladies and gentlemen, and now Conrad Nagle, a name to con*jure* with.' And that was the end of that. A few weeks later I shot the scene with Conrad where he says, 'Jack, I hate to correct you in front of an audience, but you do not pronounce that word con*jure*, it's pronounced *con*jure.' And we did a bit with some laughs in it. We shot the scene and I forgot all about it. So I got to the opening, the big Hollywood premiere at Grauman's Chinese Theater on Hollywood Boulevard. I'm watching the film and see that they cut *out* the scene when he corrects my pronunciation. And I'm stuck with that lousy word. The picture opens in New York and it's a big hit. But the New York *Times* says, 'Jack Benny, as master of ceremonies, was very funny, but if he intends to stay in the movies, it would be well worth his while to be able to speak the English language.' That was my introduction to movies.

"My second one was initially called 'Chasing Rainbows,' but they changed the title to 'Road Show.' Why, I don't know. The big hit song in that picture was 'Happy Days Are Here Again.' Now, the studio *hated* that song so much they did not want it in the picture and cut it out. The director begged them to put it back in, so they left it in for the opening and that's all. Well, it became the biggest song in the country."

The pictures were successful and his services were in demand. But the films were being done so quickly that half the time he didn't know what script he was shooting from one day to the next. Sometimes neither did the director.

"Here's the kind of thing that went on. I was doing 'The Medicine Man'—I was playing a carnival man. I was supposed to be very honest, never allowed to shortchange or cheat any of the customers. There's a scene where I'm coming out of my tent and I see two fellows talking, and I'm afraid they're planning something crooked. I walk over to talk with them. We must have rehearsed this scene six times, and each time we rehearsed it, I came striding quickly out of the tent, smiling and whistling. Nobody says anything to me about how I'm playing it. Finally, we are ready to shoot and I went to the director and said, 'By the way, what happens in the tent before I come out whistling? Maybe there's a reason for me coming out like this, or maybe there isn't.'

"He called over the script girl to find out what I was doing *in* the tent before this entrance. The female lead was supposed to be a movie star and I'm in love with her, and I'm always giving her money and gifts. In the scene prior to the one we were rehearsing, she comes into the tent to tell me she never did love me, she's always hated me, that all the money I'd given her she just gave to her other boyfriend, and then she spits at me and walks out of the tent. Now, if I hadn't spoken to the director, the awful scene in the tent would have taken place and I, in the next scene, would have come out smiling and whistling, after she'd spat on me.

"That's why a script girl is very, very important in movies or in television; she has to know exactly what happens every second. They have to remember where you were and what you did in the last take, for continuity. We had a script girl on our television show named Eula. I was doing a show with Irene Dunne, Vincent Price and Claudette Colbert. We were just about ready to resume shooting a sketch when the script girl stopped us.

" 'Just a minute. At the last take, Mr. Price, you had your hand in your left pocket, so that's where you must have it when you shoot this next scene.' We were doing this in front of a live audience, and I thought I would be a real show-off, real smart, and get a laugh. So I said loudly to the girl, in front of this large audience, 'I believe I was picking my nose at the time.' Without pause, she replied, 'No, you were through.' "

Jack relished retelling the funny little details of moviemaking. I'm sure one of the reasons he had such a long, successful and happy career was that just about everything he did amused him. When things went wrong, he laughed and moved forward, such as during the filming of "Charley's Aunt." When films are being shot with highly paid stars in the cast, studios are careful about using them in any sequence where injury is possible. If a star gets hurt and the picture is forced to shut down, hundreds of thousands of dollars can be lost daily in interest payments on the loans used to finance the film. That's why stunt men are as much a part of moviemaking as the stars.

In those classic westerns where you saw Gene Autry flying off a cliff or Roy Rogers leaping onto a moving stagecoach, you can bet you were looking at a highly skilled stunt man instead.

"Making 'Charley's Aunt,'" Jack recalled, "there was a scene when I got dressed up as the aunt, and Edmund Gwenn was supposed to fall in love with me, chasing me all around the campus, and finally we were to bump into each other, a real big crash, as a climax to the chase. Naturally, the studio was so concerned by the scene that they used two stunt men, so Edmund and I would not get hurt. All they asked me to do was come in once they were on the ground, turn and get up. That was all I had to do in the scene. Get up from the ground. So the stunt men did their chase and crash, and I did my part. Getting up from the ground I sprained my back and couldn't work for three days."

Everyone who has appeared in movies has a story about the great part that got away. My movie career consisted mostly of Warner Brothers trying to keep me *out* of their films, but Jack was a big star for Warners, and he wanted the lead in one of their epics, "Yankee Doodle Dandy," and he tried talking his way into it. Jack told me:

"'George Washington Slept Here' was a good movie and made a lot of money, so Jack Warner immediately wanted me to make another picture. He didn't care whether it was good or bad, he wanted me to make one right away. So he gave me the script of 'The Horn Blows at Midnight.' I read it and hated it. I told him, 'This is a terrible script. This is going to take months to fix up. 'George Washington Slept Here' was a good film, so let's make *another* good one.'

"Jack Warner said: ' "The Horn Blows at Midnight" will be great. And if you do it for me, I'll give you the lead in that picture about George M. If you make *this* picture I'll give you "Yankee Doodle Dandy." '

"I thought that was a pretty good trade. I finished 'The Horn Blows at Midnight,' this lousy picture, and soon found out they were already making 'Yankee Doodle Dandy' with Jimmy Cagney. I went right to Jack Warner and said, 'Wait one minute. You *prom*ised if I made that crummy picture I could play George M. Cohn!'

" 'That's Co*han*,' Warner said, smiling. 'If it was Cohn, you would have gotten it.' "

What film did Jack Benny consider his best? " 'To Be or Not to Be' was the best picture I ever made, and I'll tell you why. I had nothing to do with it being so good. And it was probably one of the greatest comedies ever made. The reason is because Ernst Lubitsch directed it. In those days, a comedian could not get a good director. But it happened that Lubitsch had the script, and he wanted me to play the part, along with Carole Lombard. One day while making the picture I was having lunch with Lubitsch. 'How did it happen you wanted me in such a dramatic comedy, when you had so many big movie stars to choose from. Why did you want me?'

"He said, 'I tell you why, Jack. You're supposed to be a fine comedian, but you're also supposed to be a lousy actor. So if you're good in my movie, *I'll* get all the credit.' "

Well, as Jack was fond of saying, it doesn't matter who says the line, as long as it gets a laugh.

My last memory of Jack comes from an evening during an Easter weekend in Palm Springs. I was spending a few days in the desert with my wife, Julann, son Tony and niece Candy. Jack was living there at the time and invited us over for Easter dinner. He took us to a small restaurant, and seated Tony and Candy on either side of him. It was a long, relaxed dinner, and the two kids, who were eight or nine at the time, both dozed off, each resting their head on Jack's shoulders. We wanted to move the kids, but Jack wouldn't hear of it. He was thrilled by it. And he insisted on finishing his dinner. He barely moved his arms, he didn't want to disturb the kids. And in doing so, he looked like the happiest man on earth.

ORSON WELLES (I)
Magic, Illusions, Miracles

THE BEST WAY I can describe my interviewing technique is to say that it is organized improvisation. Every guest who appears on my show is researched by my staff, pre-interviewed for pertinent facts about his or her current activities, and then just prior to showtime the talent coordinator responsible for a particular guest's appearance gives me a quick briefing. Details are important to me. If a guest arrives at our studio and asks to be taken to a quiet spot for a few moments of meditation before taping, or if someone wants to go immediately to the green room, where he can be surrounded by other people and commotion, these facts are relayed to me; five minutes into an interview and that information might prove useful.

Never has a guest's first appearance on my show been more thoroughly researched than that of Orson Welles and, surprisingly, never has the research proved so useless. Now I'll tell you why.

Actually, Orson *first* appeared on my show without my ever meeting him. That was 1967, when he was living in Spain; he filmed responses to some questions we had sent with a writer. At the time he had no particular plans for returning to Hollywood.

"Hollywood is a television town now," he told our writer,

27

"not a movie town, and it's less crazy and, maybe, less fun because of it. The town makes more *sense* now, and there's a sort of gray flannel shadow of Madison Avenue that's fallen over it. It's more respectable and less screwball. I kind of liked it at its worst. Here, in Europe, is where we can do our films much more economically right now, so this is where I am."

But Orson did return to the town that had vilified him—the Hearst press kept his name out of their papers for years following "Citizen Kane"—and finally, in 1976, arrangements were made for our first in-person interview. We decided to devote an entire show to him, ninety minutes of a one-on-one interview. To prepare for the meeting, I assigned my top talent coordinator, Paul Solomon, to spend two weeks researching Welles's life and career.

We don't always have the luxury of time. In 1965 I was in Cannes with a small crew to film star interviews from the Cannes Film Festival. One afternoon I was down near the beach when someone told me he'd seen John Lennon sunning himself. I looked in the direction where I was told Lennon was sitting, but it seemed unlikely he was there. This was at the height of Beatlemania, and if Lennon was on the beach, he would be causing nothing but chaos. We walked along the beach and, sure enough, there he was, reading a book and getting a tan. I introduced myself—he had a vague idea that I was somebody of note from American television—and he readily agreed to do an interview, his first for an American talk show. There wasn't any time for preparation, but we did a delightful few minutes together, and we took our treasure back to America.

With the Welles interview we had the luxury of time. My staff turned libraries inside out, obtained permissions to show clips from the Welles film archives and gathered still photographs to illustrate the scope of his career. By tape day I knew as much about Orson Welles as any one could learn from print, and I felt fully prepared to host one of the most complete retrospectives of an artist's life we had ever attempted on "The Merv Griffin Show."

I was soon to get my first lesson in the importance of being Orson Welles.

Paul Solomon walked into the office of my producer, Bob Murphy, on the afternoon prior to our taping, looking shaken. He'd just spoken with Mr. Welles. "There won't be any trips down memory lane with *this* guy," Paul announced. Evidently, when he called Orson to explain the details of our retrospective, Welles became enraged, delivering a barrage of four-letter words that Solomon had not heard since he had interviewed Rocky Graziano, the boxer.

"I live for now, *today,*" Orson shouted at him, "I don't want to rehash goddamn old news!"

I got the word a couple of hours before tape time, and was facing ninety minutes with a cinema genius who had led a front-page life, but who didn't want to talk about either subject. Wonderful.

However, if my first lesson in the Orson Welles mystique taught me that he doesn't enjoy talking about his past (a habit he's changed for the benefit of my show), the second, which came during the taping, was more rewarding. Since I couldn't directly use our research, I threw topics from the news and current events at him, and learned what I suppose his friends already knew: regardless of the subject, Orson comes equipped with witty, erudite and colorful conversation. As the French artist and man of letters Jean Cocteau once said, "Orson Welles is a giant with a child's face, a tree inhabited by birds, a dog who has broken his chains to sleep on a bed of flowers."

At lunch with him one afternoon I brought up his reluctance to speak of the past, and by way of answering he likened memories to cities. "I feel at home almost everywhere," he said, "but there are places you shouldn't go back to. That great saying, 'You can't go home again,' certainly applies to me. Ireland I won't go back to. I have a right to say that because two of the happiest years of my life were spent there, and my dearest friends in the world are there. And the last time I went back to that beautiful country it had begun to be destroyed by imitation Detroits and Chicagos. Bad buildings had begun to rise in Dublin. Friends had died and gone. That's what I mean by not going back. I want to love the Ireland I *left*. Just as I don't want to go back to Brazil, where I spent a year in the early forties, and I don't want to go back because it will be a different Brazil, and I'm not *ready* for a different Brazil. Once I fall in love with a place I'm not in love with it after it's changed; I have not found anywhere in the world that is better than it was."

This is not just an intellectual pose, it is a way of life for him. He told me that since the presidency of his friend Franklin Roosevelt he has refused numerous invitations to visit the White House. "I didn't want to go back to it because it used to look like a country house, old-fashioned, the kind of place where you'd open a door somewhere and a tennis racket and an old golf club would fall out. It was somebody's house. But ever since Jackie Onassis redecorated it so that it looks like an expensive Sheraton hotel, well . . ."

With this attitude in mind, Orson told me he planned *not* to write his autobiography, to let the pleasant parts of his past stay where they are, and to move on with his life. But as we grew comfortable with each other, a dialogue opened up, and so did Orson. In the many appearances he has made on my show, following that confusing first one, he has shared some pieces of his rich and unusual life. I'd like to gather some of his memories now, and share them with you.

I can trace my own beginnings in the entertainment busi-ness to back porch shows I used to stage for kids in the neighborhood, Saturday afternoon events with little substance and much drama. Orson links his beginnings as an actor to a trip he took to Ireland when he was only fifteen years old.

"I was planning to spend two weeks in Ireland, and then go to Scotland for the rest of the summer to paint; at the time I fully intended to be a painter. My father had just died, he had left me a few hundred dollars, and I was going to spend it as a painter. I had won a scholarship to Harvard, but there was nothing in the world I wanted to do less than go back to school, so I was looking for other work as I was wandering around Ireland. I bought a donkey and a cart and I traveled around the country, painting, and at night I slept beneath the cart. I traveled with tinkers—gypsies—for a couple of weeks, but they stole too many of my paintings. In fact, I have very few of those paintings left, because when it rained I was always invited in by an Irish family—the hospitality of Ireland, as you know, is incredible—and I was always given dinner and a warm place to sleep. My hosts would then ask for a painting, so by the end of my trip I didn't have many left. Finally I took a barge and went from the mouth of the Shannon River to the source. I took a bicycle with me, so when the scenery became dull I'd bicycle on ahead, wait for the barge and reboard. That brought me near enough to take a train into Dublin.

"I had about four pounds left by then, and I blew it on a theater ticket. I went to see this play and in it was an extra I'd met elsewhere, a young Trinity student, and I went backstage to greet him. He introduced me to the directors of the theater, and I heard myself saying—I had only two pounds left, and *didn't* want to go back to Harvard—that I was a famous actor from the New York Theater Guild, and that I could be persuaded, for amusement's sake, to stay on in Dublin for a while *if* there were any leading roles.

"Of course, I'd never been on a stage and never seriously intended to be an actor. They did have a leading role in a production they hadn't cast, but they said would I mind terribly reading for them. 'We know, of course, who you are, but would you mind?' Well, they had never *heard* of me. By then I was fifteen, smoking to look older, and using a deep voice I'd practiced to persuade people to serve me in pubs. So I read for them and got the part—it was an historical drama. The show had five acts in it, and in each act the lead gets older. In one he rapes a girl (offstage), in another he has apoplexy, and he ends up dying on his throne. It *had* to be the biggest success in the world. And I didn't give a damn what happened, so I just got up there on stage and hammered away. Well, because of my profound ignorance, I got the ovations and notices of my life. And my career as an actor was off and running."

Orson shares some personal history with a surprisingly large number of the gifted writers and actors, painters and politicians who have appeared on my show over the years. Time and again I have heard from these people that early in their lives they suffered the loss of one or both parents. I hear it often enough to call it a pattern. Why parental loss is often a precursor to exceptional talent is a question better left to psychologists, but one might suggest that the loss of a parent leaves a void often filled, or perhaps replaced, by a remarkable career. Orson Welles lost both parents by the time he was a teenager, but he vividly recalls their influence on him.

"I was very lucky," he says, "because I had parents who took me to the theater when I could hardly sit on a lap. As a child I had an adult vocabulary because I stayed up late at night and listened to grownups. You see, I was a kind of third-rate musical wunderkind, playing piano and violin, and I conducted too. And that kept me up with the adults at night, because my mother's great friends were distinguished musicians. She died when I was eight, and I never played music again; it was a very traumatic thing for me.

"I wasn't really all *that* bright, but I was told by my mother that I was, so I damn well had to be. As a reader, I learned by memorizing from 'A Midsummer Night's Dream,' and that was rough going. But that was the way it was with my mother; she wasn't going to stand for any nonsense. My father died when I was fourteen and a half. He was a remarkable man and an eccentric of the first order. He was a friend to show people. In the last years of his life he ran a hotel in a town with a population of 120. He bought the hotel—in fact he bought the whole town. It had been a staging area for the covered wagons. He hired people only from small-time show business. We had a woman who did bird calls as our waitress, and our handyman was a 'rattlesnake-oil' pitchman who had worked in medicine shows. There were all kinds of people like that. My father was mad about magic, and when I was six years old he introduced me to Houdini.

"My other relatives were southerners, mad, mad, southerners. I had a lot of great aunts who were mad. I had one aunt who rode the Jamestown flood on a piano. It's one of those stories you hear in your family, and you repeat it to get a laugh, without really believing it. When I told it once before I received a letter from a very old lady who said she was in Jamestown during the flood and saw another lady floating down Main Street atop a grand piano. That must have been my dear Aunt Grace.

"Then there was my Aunt Hat, who always wore riding britches and a bright red wig, which she took off to salute you. She would slap her thigh and shout, 'That's the ticket!' Once she wanted to go on a diet. She owned an electric car and would instruct her chauffeur to tie her to the back, drive her out to the country, and she would run along behind the car. Once the rope broke and the chauffeur never looked back; she was lost in the country for hours.

"Another aunt of mine disappeared in a rickshaw in Nanking, in China. Now, *I* don't believe this, but my family always told the story. My old grandmother, who was a witch, and her sister were riding in this rickshaw. The coolies in front got involved in some kind of altercation, threw up their traces, and these two old ladies fell into a crowd of turbulent Chinese, and only grandmother survived. The great aunt was never heard from again. Carried off into white slavery, perhaps.

"But my mother was an absolutely marvelous woman. She was a suffragette, a radical who spent time in jail as a peace demonstrator. She was also a national champion rifle shot and a concert pianist. *And* a fabulous beauty. If I had had the chance of knowing her longer, it would have been a great boon, indeed."

Mention Orson Welles's name at a party and the first words you'll hear are "Citizen Kane." We'll get into Orson's film career a little later on. But right now let's talk about the second thing people will mention in connection with Orson: "The War of the Worlds" radio broadcast. It's tough for young people to believe a radio broadcast could have scared the hell out of the United States of America, but that is in fact what happened. It was almost as if Walter Cronkite had come on television and announced a Martian invasion. But to Orson, it was a simple prank that got way out of hand.

"It was Halloween," he remembers, "and it was my way of soaping a window, as I said at the end of the broadcast, although by that time everybody was out with towels on their wet heads, running and screaming through the streets. At the end of the program I said, 'This is our way of soaping your windows and saying *boo!*' Things were quite out of control by then. To the extent that I met some Quakers, years later, who had spent five weeks in the Ozark mountains persuading people to come down out of the hills, and having a hell of a hard time convincing them that the Martians weren't *really* marching down Fifth Avenue.

"Of all the reactions to the broadcast, my favorite is Jack Barrymore's. He believed every word of the broadcast. He later told me that when it came to the moment the Martians were striding down Madison Avenue, he went outside to his kennel, where there were twenty St. Bernards, opened the gates and shouted, 'Fend for yourselves!' "

That may have been Welles's greatest illusion in a lifelong fascination with illusion, magic and the seemingly miraculous. Many people forget that Orson actually had a stage show that toured the country, displaying stunning magical tricks, and assisted by two of the world's most glamorous women, Marlene Dietrich and Rita Hayworth. Orson's meeting with Harry Houdini, when he was six years old, obviously had its impact. Even today he enjoys performing small illusions on my show. They are not, however, improvised bits. When Orson announces he is going to do a trick on the show, we schedule a rehearsal during which he demonstrates each part of the performance for my director, Dick Carson, so that the cameras always catch the essential moves. Many times I've assisted him in a trick, I've had my nose right in the middle of it, and I'm still baffled by some of his performances.

He learned from the master of all time.

"Houdini is a hero to me. He taught me the 'pass,' which is the first move in card magic, backstage at the Palace Theater in New York. The man was the highest paid vaudeville act in the history of show business. A lot of old-time magicians put the rap on Houdini, because he wasn't terribly nice to other magicians. And they never wasted an opportunity to get even with him. I remember when a group of magicians in London gave Houdini a dinner, an evening of tribute, and in the middle of the evening the lights went out; a fuse had blown. So they all took candles and went down to the cellar to the fuse box.

It had a padlock, which Houdini volunteered to open. With all these magicians standing around, he started tinkering with it but simply couldn't get it open. What he didn't know is that they had gaffed it so it *wouldn't* open. A small piece of revenge on their part.

"But Houdini challenged anybody, and he could get out of *anything*, always. Just think of his last great illusion, suspending himself upside down in a tank of water, chained and strait-jacketed. It took an awful lot of nerve, but he did it for several years. It was a challenge. A yogi would come into the country and be buried alive for the benefit of the press. Houdini would say, *'I* can do that,' not knowing whether or not he actually could. So he had himself put into a lead casket and lowered to the bottom of the Sheraton hotel swimming pool, and stayed down there for five hours and, obviously, came up alive. He just figured if he did shallow breathing he'd live through it. That's *chutzpah.*"

I had always heard that elaborate attempts were made after Houdini's death to reach him by means of mediums and psychics, employing specific instructions left by Houdini himself. "Tremendous attempts *were* made," Orson confirmed. "He spent a lot of time near the end of his life exposing fraudulent spiritualist mediums, who were then in very big power; they were what astrologers are now (psychiatrists and yogis, too, for that matter). Everybody seemed to believe in those mediums, and Houdini knew how to expose them. And the *reason* he tried so hard to do so was that he had to be the biggest mama's boy who ever lived. The night his mother was buried, he spent the entire night lying flat on her grave, that's how broken up he was. And his attempts to expose mediums really came from the fact that he wanted to find a legitimate one. And never did.

"People gave fortunes in those days to mediums; it was a very big racket. I exposed some of them myself. In Mexico there was a famous magician named Mamburg, who came from seven generations of Dutch magicians; he worked as a Chinese in Mexico, using a Chinese accent though speaking Spanish, after having been raised in Brooklyn. I exposed his chicanery. In fact, every psychic I've attempted to expose *has* been a fake. The real psychics, the ones who impressed me the most, are simple people who live in native villages and are called 'witches,' 'wise women' or 'wizards.' That's the closest I've come to seeing the real thing.

"We're discovering that the so-called sciences of psychology and psychiatry are increasingly being exposed, too, for being inexact—they are coming closer to the paranormal. More and more 'scientific' disciplines are taking the paranormal seriously. But it is an unknown area, one in which it is awfully easy to fall into the hands of crooks. But don't be frightened by the occult, psychics, flying saucers, any of that, not for one minute. Better be frightened of all those bad movies about these things. I believe it is like electricity *before* we understood it; when you comb your hair there might be sparks and your hair would stick to the comb . . . miraculous, until we learned about static electricity. And that's about all the occult has going for it. We'll soon learn more and won't be frightened by it.

"Take flying saucers; there are enough reports about them, and I think there *is* something to it. But whatever people are seeing is a projection of the era we live in. For example, there's the ancient theory that all the fiery chariots our ancestors saw in the sky were really flying saucers. But people then saw them as chariots; they didn't see saucers. Because in those times chariots were common, an everyday sight, and saucers were not. Today people see flying saucers because that's what our culture and technology project. Whatever people absorb, that is what is translated to their eyes, and that is what they report 'seeing.' "

There is more to the story of UFOs, however, than Orson reports. Naturally, talk shows attract every kind of sensationalist who is ready to claim he'd been abducted by space aliens, but we weed out those types effectively. There is a growing body of evidence, advanced by respected scientists, that indicates not only are there "flying saucers" up there but that some have, indeed, landed. Former astronaut Gordon Cooper told me once during his stint as an Air Force pilot he encountered UFOs—that is, airborne objects that moved unlike any aircraft built by man. He contends that other astronauts and Air Force pilots feel exactly as he does, with similar experiences in their logs, but are timid about discussing them for fear of being labeled crackpots or publicity seekers.

Now, as regards psychic experiences, I don't think there is any doubt that the vast majority of reported experiences have little scientific merit. But I'm sure that some do. Convincing evidence comes from the medical community, respected members of which have reported startling experiences with patients who have been pronounced clinically dead, were revived and came to recount complicated surgical procedures occurring during the period of their "death." "After-death" patients have even reported verbatim conversations held in the intensive care room, all of which seemingly occurred during the period of unconsciousness. The evidence is simply too substantial not to recognize and respect it. When it comes to people being "possessed" by spirits and living in haunted houses, that is another matter. Orson told me he witnessed an exorcism on his first trip to Ireland.

"I was in Innishere, and saw a very old house being moved, stone by stone, across the road from its original site; the reasons for the move were explained to me in Gaelic, so I never fully understood them. Somebody they called 'the little red man' lived in the house. The house stood open in the fields as it was being moved and reconstructed. Evidently there was a room inside that had been sealed in order to trap an evil spirit. When the villagers started to move the stones, the old man slept against the back part of the wall of this room. A stone fell on him and hurt his leg. So he called on the village priest to exorcise the spirit, put it back into the room and reseal it.

"I was fascinated and remained to witness the result. A young, well-educated and intelligent priest arrived, deeply embarrassed to see me there, knowing he had to go through with the ceremony for the old man's peace of mind. I learned from him that a priest is not obligated to *believe* the evil spirit was going back into the room, but it obviously gave comfort to the victim. So, in fact, I saw the 'bell, book and candle' ceremony and the resealing of the room. The evil spirit didn't materialize to spin his head around, as they do in the movies. But everyone in the village was convinced that the spirit went back into the room, trapped once again. The priest made an attempt to convince them that once a spirit is exorcised it is gone forever, but that was a fine point the locals weren't prepared to recognize. And that one room still stands, across the road from the rest of the house."

*

SOPHIA LOREN:
"I like to be by myself. I like to be alone, because when I'm working I am among so many people that after work is over I like to be at home with my family. I like to think, to talk to myself, think about what I will do next. I keep myself good company."

*

One of my pet subjects is greatness: great people and their accomplishments. It is a mercurial quality, especially in these times of three-paragraph profiles in People and the saturation of the electronic media. People today rarely seem to have enough *privacy* to cultivate the qualities of greatness, much less sustain these qualities. This is a subject Orson Welles is in a position to discuss, because not only has he studied history for his entire life, but he had known many of the people—Winston Churchill, Franklin Roosevelt—whom modern historians consider "great."

"I think greatness," he observes, "by some strange law never appears among leaders in a bland period of history. Think of all the great men who arrived in America at the time of the Civil War, great men on both sides, military leaders whose tactics are still taught in Europe, to be compared with those of Napoleon. Men with personalities you couldn't believe—quite apart from Lincoln, who was himself a towering man, one of the greatest who ever lived. And these people never could have surfaced if the country hadn't been torn apart. They were real heroes, not manufactured ones like our astronauts, those chamber of commerce men in comic costumes. I suppose the last real American *hero* was Lindbergh. He represented America in every sense; he was a loner, a pioneer, reflecting in his effort the things we like to think about as our national identity. There was much more technology guiding our astronauts to the moon than there was taking Lindy across the Atlantic Ocean.

"Latent greatness exists in certain people, and the times bring it out. Churchill was almost sixty before his call to greatness came; and then it was four years the like of which will never be known again. The greatness is already there, but the times call it forth. I am convinced there is much greatness in people, people who *could* be great if opportunity provided them with that chance. There are so many great actors getting on the bus each day and going to work at the factory or a bank, and they will never act. Writers who have never sat down to write . . . how many fine writers we know who didn't *start* to write until they were fifty or sixty years old. Perhaps the greatest novel ever written is *Don Quixote;* it was written by Cervantes only because he was put in jail in his late fifties. He never would have written a thing of value without that experience.

We have *it,* but we require time and chemistry to bring it out."

In my own experience, I would put Gerald R. Ford in the category Orson is speaking of. Here is a man who served in the Congress for decades, respected but hardly a national figure. Then his call to greatness came when he was made Vice-President and, suddenly, President of the United States. He arrived during a most precarious time in American history. We were reeling from the impact of Watergate and the economic aftershocks of the Vietnam war. And this quiet, down-to-earth public servant went about putting the country back into order, stabilizing us. He represents the classic case of a man meeting the challenge of his times, not on a scale with the deeds of Churchill, but important nonetheless.

Orson's favorite encounter with Winston Churchill came after the English leader's "period of greatness."

"I was in Venice, trying to raise money for a movie. I had a pigeon with me, a Russian man of mystery reputed to have a billion dollars; I wanted to part him from a small portion of that money to make my film. So I was busy trying to impress him with my importance. Churchill was staying with his wife at the same hotel.

"We came into lunch, my Russian angel and myself, one particular afternoon, and as we entered the dining room we passed Mr. and Mrs. Churchill. As I passed, he nodded to me. Now, I don't know if he truly remembered me; we'd met a few times before. Anyway, he knew I was *some* kind of person, and he politely nodded. My pigeon was *so* impressed. He said, 'My goodness, Mr. Churchill *knows* you.'

"I nodded nonchalantly, 'Yes, of course.'

"Next day, about eleven in the morning, I took a swim and found myself on the beach next to Churchill. I said to him, 'You don't know what you did for me, sir. When I came into the dining room yesterday with this man—I'm trying to raise money for a film—and you nodded to me, you've no idea how much that helped me. I just want to thank you.' He didn't say anything, because he was deaf, and often used that ploy for privacy—you never knew whether he had heard you or not. I thought maybe I'd gone too far with him. I left to shower and dress for lunch. At the appointed hour I met my Russian, with whom I was still negotiating, and we went to the dining room. And once again there sat Mr. and Mrs. Churchill. As we passed the table Churchill looked slyly at me and winked. I got the money and made the film."

When I'm asked to choose my favorite performances ever by an actor and actress, I think of three. For the actor it is a draw between Montgomery Clift and Marlon Brando. Clift for "A Place in the Sun" and Brando for his Broadway run in *A Streetcar Named Desire*. Monty Clift brought an intensity to his work that was rare and completely controlled. Brando in *Streetcar* redefined for me the paramaters of acting, such was the dimension of his performance. For a favorite actress I choose Gene Tierney in "Laura," in which she gave a performance heightened by a sense of vulnerability; she made me want to leap through the screen to assist her.

For Orson, acting begins and ends with a man today's generation will barely recognize, John Barrymore. "I knew all the Barrymores very well," Orson says, "and John was the greatest. As a youth, I stood in the wings of a theater with a bucket of champagne for Jack Barrymore to take sips in between scenes of "Hamlet." When he was on pitch and in command of himself, when he *wanted* to be, he was the greatest. And the irony was he didn't want to *be* an actor. That was his tragedy, because he was born to be the greatest actor of the century."

The last part of Barrymore's life, I mentioned to Orson, was littered with stories of public drunkenness and a string of truly bad movies; it was hard for me to go along with Orson's assessment of greatness. But Orson offered some reasons behind this checkered period of John Barrymore's life.

"You have to understand that his father—a great matinee idol, Maurice Barrymore—died in a madhouse. His father went absolutely mad on the stage, and was taken to the laughing academy. Poor Jack would lose his way and not know how he got to the studio, and he would use the fact that he liked to drink, pretending to be *very* drunk, to mask the thought of going down the same path as his father. He played the drunk to hide his terror of madness. That's the real truth about him. And he played in all those bad movies at the end in order to pay his creditors. I knew him as a great gentleman, a wonderful man. And if you want to know what he was truly like, check out "Grand Hotel," and the character he plays in that is much of what he really was, a simple, gentlemanly fellow."

Orson is not quite ready to canonize him, however. "He could be a bit of a devil. I chose him to accompany me to the opening of my first movie at Grauman's Chinese Theater in Hollywood, because I worshipped his acting and thought it would be a thrill to have him along. This was in the days when we still had the big crowds at premiers, with bleachers, and the announcer shouting, 'Here comes Norma Shearer's car!' As you entered the theater you'd stop and say a few words to the national radio audience. So we arrived and the announcer said, 'Here's Mr. John Barrymore with Orson Welles, who made the picture.' As we approached he asked, 'What do you have to say on this occasion, Mr. Barrymore?'

" 'Now it can be told,' Jack began, as I started shrinking into my shoes, 'Orson Welles is, in fact, the bastard son of my sister Ethel and the Pope.'

"You can bet that broadcast was cut off the air in a hurry. Another time Jack and I were having lunch at the Brown

Derby . . . I'm going to use the word bleep in place of myriad profanities . . . and I was asking Jack why he had married his current wife.

" 'I'll tell you, Orson,' he began, leaning forward, 'because she has bleep, bleep, bleep, bleeping bleeps and bleep,' and continued on with this unbelievably ribald description of his wife's charms. Well, I could see that a man at the next booth, with his wife and children, obviously tourists from some small Indiana town, was quite shocked at what he was overhearing. He summoned the headwaiter and complained, but the waiter only shrugged as the barrage of bleeps continued from our table. The man then got up and went outside. I watched through a window as he flagged down a policeman and brought him back in. So this flotilla—the angry man, the policeman, the headwaiter and several busboys—approached our table. They stopped just in back of Barrymore, and the man said, 'Mr. Barrymore, I've come all the way from Indiana with my wife and children to see Hollywood, and if this is your idea how a famous actor . . .'

"During this speech Jack goes right on talking to me, unaware, 'And, Orson . . . her bleep is so incredibly . . .'

"But the other man pressed on: 'Mr. Barrymore, we have always looked up to motion picture people, but I assure you . . .'

" 'Bleeping girl has bleep for . . .'

"Finally I got Jack's attention by pointing directly at the assemblage standing behind him. He turned around and looked at the man in front of the cop. Jack looked quite surprised and turned to me. 'What is this? A peasant with a petition?'

"I didn't stop laughing for two days."

Often when you hear stories about Hollywood's greats, you are hearing stories of underlying tragedies—John Barrymore,

Marilyn Monroe, Montgomery Clift—the list could stretch for pages. Orson has ventured the opinion that we place movie stars in the pantheon where the ancient Greeks placed their gods, and observe them in the same fashion the Greeks did.

"I think the great ones *are* godlike, in the Greek sense, because the gods in the Greek pantheon are full of frailties; they are lechers and drunkards and make terrible mistakes, yet they are gods. So in that sense, because those gods are larger than life, their frailty doesn't change the strangely godlike aspect someone like Chaplin or Barrymore had. That *quality* was inextinguishable. I recall going to Chicago to be present at Jack's deathbed. Ethel and Lionel Barrymore had arrived— they hadn't seen Jack in years—and we all gathered in Chicago. However, we couldn't *find* Jack, ill as he might have been. It turned out he was in some house of ill fame on the South Side, and we had a lot of trouble getting back in order to have a deathbed scene, which he refused to do for a couple more years. Here was the classic case of the crown prince who didn't want to be king.

"Here were all these great actors in the Barrymore family, stretching back for generations, and he had inherited this tremendous gift, which he simply didn't want. Yet he was forced into being a great actor, because God meant him to be. So he went kicking and screaming into it, and found his way out through Hollywood self-indulgence and alcohol. But, by God, he did it with great gallantry."

Orson Welles is a great admirer of women, and many great women have admired *him.* However, it is the one subject you won't get him to discuss. But for a star of the stature of Marlene Dietrich to travel with Orson simply to be an extra in his magic show demonstrates the marvelous appeal of the man.

"I've known some exceptional ladies," Orson once told me, "but never the kind who appear unsympathetically in movies as nagging wives or girl friends. I've only known very superior ladies and my debt to them is beyond speech. You see, the sad thing about men is we can't get along without women. And the even sadder fact is, it turns out, they can get along awfully well without us. Pretty soon we're going to revert to what we were initially in a biological sense, we're going to have little function at all. Babies are going to be made in bottles, the ladies are going to make money, dishes are going to be done by machinery . . . it's difficult to figure out what our place will be."

*

FRANK CAPRA—On working with leading ladies:
"As a director, you've got to fall in love with your leading ladies. When you work for weeks, perhaps months, with some beautiful girl, you're closer to her and get to know her better than even her family. And she knows you too, better than anybody knows you, because it's a very intense moment when you're communicating in trying to play a part. You talk about it in every way. You look at her through a camera and she gets more beautiful every day you see her. And something happens; you fall in love, perhaps not with the actress, but with the part that the actress is playing. And you've got to be very professional about this, as this can lead into places where you shouldn't go."

*

Despite that gloomy prediction, men will have a place as long as they retain the romantic attitude Orson exhibited in his early life. One of the monuments to his romantic nature stands along the Pacific Coast in Big Sur, not far from my home in Carmel Valley. He built a glorious home there as a romantic retreat for himself and Rita Hayworth.

"She made slipcovers and curtains and worked hard to put things in the house," Orson recalls, "but when it came to spending the night, her Spanish blood showed, because Latins don't like to live all alone in the country; they like to be where other people are. Ventanna in Big Sur was then a paradise, nothing but deer and open country. We never spent a night there, however. When it came to Rita and me parting the ways we sold the house. In the meantime, the writer Henry Miller lived there for several years without asking our permission or even paying any rent. That distinguished author was a squatter in our house. We were happy to hear about it."

He does tell one story about his tour with Marlene. She knew Orson was acquainted with Greta Garbo, Dietrich's favorite actress, and for months begged Orson to arrange an introduction.

"So I got Clifton Webb to give a party and we didn't warn Garbo that Dietrich would also be there. I arrived with Marlene, who approached Garbo immediately and said, 'You're the greatest actress who ever lived and I am at your feet and I worship you.' But Garbo was very cold and just gave Marlene a snotty look. Marlene, undaunted, went right on praising her. When the party dwindled I took Marlene home. We were driving through the hills and she was quiet for some time. Finally she said, as if she had been thinking about it for quite a while, 'You know, Orson, Garbo's feet aren't as big as people say they are.' "

Orson not only admires women, he even admires the aesthetics of their fashions. "In fact, I would have loved to have been a women's dress designer," he told me. "You may make of that what you will. I used to go to the openings in Paris in the days when there were *real* dress designers; and I maintain that there aren't any now. I used to go to the great showings, not with any purpose in mind, but for the pleasure of looking. Today's designers can't sew; they're just masters of media. I don't think that women's clothes are any use at all nowadays; I don't think there is a fashion. There are, of course, economic reasons for that, because women can't afford fashion. And there is simply nobody who knows how to sew and cut like a master, in the class of Chanel.

"Chanel was a real genius. She *changed* the world. Here was a poor little peasant girl, not very pretty, who caught the eye of a rich gentleman who brought her to Paris. That was a time when women used to wear combinations of leather, lace and plumes; it was the godawfulest time for fashion. And Coco Chanel went to the races in Paris, and saw these ladies sashaying around in enormous gowns, and knew *she* would look absurd in them. So she changed the look of the entire world so that she would look good. A great Chanel dress is still like a Stradivarius. You have to admire any woman who can do what she did."

Earlier I mentioned that a common trait many successful and creative people I've met share is the early loss of a parent. Another shared trait is an obsession with time and its rapid passage. All of them feel the pressure of so many ambitions to squeeze into a short lifetime. I recall writers, such as Norman Mailer, James Michener, James Jones and Irving Stone, recounting for me lists of books they hoped to complete before death. I think of Picasso filling one house after another with art, up to the moment he died.

"I began thinking about death the minute they told me about it," Orson Welles remembers, "and I was indeed very little then. I've never *stopped* thinking about it. I fear dying before I have accomplished something that I'm not ashamed of, that I'm even a little proud of. I'm afraid I will be taken away before I have justified the luck and joy I've had being here. I don't think you are truly alive unless you constantly remember you're going to die. In fact, I think what give dignity and tragedy, meaning and beauty, to life *is* the fact that we will die. This knowledge that we will die has been with me every day of my life. And I think it is a mistake in our modern society that our idea of a good time is a plastic-enclosed, painless, deathless world, a world in which 'death' itself is an obscene word. We now use all the four-letter words in our everyday vocabulary, but not 'death': we 'pass away.' Well, we god-damned well *die*! And if we don't *know* we are going to die, nothing in life is sufficiently precious to us. It is one of the great gifts of God, if you happen to believe in Him, that we *are* going to die; it would be terrible if we weren't."

We tend to marvel at older people who are creative and productive in their seventies, eighties and nineties; it seems most of the public longs for the day when they can "retire" and relax. But I think Orson has the secret to a meaningful later life. Instead of using the knowledge that death is coming to rob one of incentive, the great people of our time use this knowledge as a motivator; there are things they want to *do* before their time is up. Every time Bob Hope gives an interview he is asked when he plans to retire. And each time he'll look at the reporter or television interviewer with a mystified expression and say, "Retire to *what?* I'm having fun." I'll always remember speaking with the historian Will Durant, the author of *The Story of Civilization,* when he was in his early nineties. He had a lengthy list of subjects he wanted to learn about, and expressed hope he could satisfy his curiosity in these areas before he died.

Orson tells a marvelous story about one man's confrontation with sudden mortality. "I was on a plane flight some years ago, seated next to a United States senator. Our plane got into a terrible storm, an engine went out, and clearly we were going to crash. The pilot was desperately searching for a field in which to land—in these days planes could still do that. As the trouble worsened, the senator began busily writing a letter. An older gentleman sitting across the aisle from me said, 'I'm very sorry about this because I have three more chapters to go in this mystery book and now I'll never know who the murderer was.'

"I thought his good humor in this desperate moment was quite wonderful. But the senator was all business. He hastily finished his letter, handed a copy to me and said, 'This is for my wife. I've written another that's in my pocket, and in case I'm burnt up in the crash . . . perhaps *you* won't be, and you'll deliver it to her for me. The letter is to explain to my wife why I'm on this plane, because I told her I wasn't going to be in Philadelphia. I told her I was going to Boston. This explains it all.' Here was a man *truly* afraid of his wife. And I said, right to his face, 'We're going to crash any minute and you're *still* explaining to her!' "

Orson views life today from the perspective of his sixties. "I think the only absolutely fatal age is middle age. I spent my youth pretending to be old and I'm getting to the time of life when I'm going to start pretending to be young. But never be middle-aged. I'm leaping nimbly out of it. Actually, I think old age is a splendid condition. I believe all the stages of life have their meaning. And the only thing wrong we do is pretend to be what we are not. Old age has its benefits, not that we have to be cheerful about it. What I'm against is that awful idleness of the old; it is a dangerous trend. Since the family has collapsed as a unit, or very nearly so, the old people are shoveled away, either because the young don't want them, or the old simply don't want to be around. In any case, we've broken up the unit.

"The old have no purpose unless they have power. It is not

love so much that keeps us going, it's power. That's why symphony conductors never die; they have that enormous orchestra in front of them, and they exercise in front of it like an
athlete. They conduct symphonies at age eighty-five and feel
fine, because they have total power. But we take this kind of
power away from our older people, the power over the family,
the power of being a wise old woman or the wise old man.
These people need a feeling of power to invest their lives with
meaning. I don't think that bingo and shuffleboard can possible
make up for the pleasures of being the head of a family."

Many film critics contend that Orson Welles has already left
us two works, "Citizen Kane" and "The Magnificent Ambersons," that are immortal. I asked him once if these are the
things he would like to be remembered by.

"I think of the immortality of an artist as a conception as
vulgar as success. To be interested in immortality is simply a
transcendental form of vainglory. I'd like to be remembered by
a few friends for anything that I did that was good. I don't
know that I really want to admit *anything* I've done is good
enough to be remembered anymore than I want to state that
it's bad enough to be lost. But we live in a time of tremendous
perishability. Not only is the planet likely to be blown up, but
the books we write are printed on paper of a nature which will
fall to pieces in forty or fifty years. The paint today's artists use
is badly made and is falling off the canvas. We now make only
color movies, and color fades, and the very color of our celluloid
will be gone in sixty or seventy years.

"So why do we all labor so, trying to create works of art? I
think we do it for the best reason in the world: for ourselves,
for the joy of the work. Anything else that comes with it is so
much gravy, and it can be beautiful gravy. But to depend on

it, to think we're building another pyramid when we write another book or make a film, is to be badly mistaken. Although who knows," Orson concluded, looking away from me, as if remembering a work of art he loved, "there may be a beautiful book or film that remains, something saved for the future. Marvelous things *do* happen."

RICHARD BURTON
A Passion for Living

THERE ARE MANY different styles of acting, but among the great practitioners of the art, I find two basic types. First, the type whose true personality is submerged beneath the roles he plays, a sort of sponge capable of absorbing another person's character and traits, of becoming someone else entirely. Often, the real personality of this type of actor is not nearly so well defined as the fictional character he portrays. In this category I include Robert DiNiro, Al Pacino, Dustin Hoffman and Jon Voight, all of whom are among the most brilliant actors of their generation, yet even their most ardent fans aren't able to get a clear portrait of them outside of their screen roles. These men are masters at capturing the emotions of a character and keeping them consistent throughout a performance; they are actors of the heart.

Then there are the actors of the mind, who approach a role with the same intense scrutiny that an archeologist brings to the study of a rare fossil. This type of actor examines a role from every angle, interprets it and, finally, knows more about the motivations of the character than a true-life counterpart could ever know unless he had spent a lifetime in analysis. Invariably the actors of this school are stars of immense personality: Katharine Hepburn, Marlon Brando, Orson Welles,

Richard Burton. As Orson Welles astutely observes, no actor can play a great villain unless there is villainy within the actor; one cannot play a king unless within the actor lurks a kingly persona.

What better example of this can be found than Richard Burton. He has played kings of gigantic dimension, as well as brooding villains. My impression is that what we see at work with him is not "playacting," but a drawing out of his tempestuous Welsh soul in synch with an imposing intellect. He exudes a passion for living that sometimes consumes him and those close to him, but this imbues him with a personality as potent as his best roles. I watched him at work on location for the film "The Klansman," shot in Oroville, California, in 1972, and believe me, Richard Burton is a high flyer unafraid of being seared by the sun.

When a movie company films in a small town like Oroville it is like an invasion of Martians; nobody on either side knows quite how to behave. The townspeople are fascinated by the process that brings movies to life, and of course by the public behavior of international stars like Richard Burton and Lee Marvin. The actors want to be friendly and well received, but they also want to go about the business of making their movie and enjoy a little time by themselves. When you are Richard Burton, however, and are married to Elizabeth Taylor, everything you do is observed, photographed, written about, commented on and, in the end, judged.

"Wouldn't it be nice," Burton said to me one afternoon between takes, "if people didn't recognize me or my wife? She's very lovely. I'm very fond of her, and I believe she's very fond of me—of course you can never tell about a woman—but wouldn't it be nice *not* to be recognized." He considered that for a moment, then added, "When they *don't* recognize you, of course, it's a nasty shock. Once we were in southwest Africa, where the latest film shown was the original version of 'King Kong.' They didn't know who Elizabeth was, they didn't know who I was. I was *surprised* at that, perhaps a little taken aback. One night I was filming with Alec Guinness and Peter Ustinov, and we stayed on long afterward, sitting in some bar, talking. Elizabeth worried where I was. She said to her hairdresser, 'Call the bars. Find out where he is.' They called around— there were only five bars in the place. The girl called the bar where we are and says, 'I would like to speak to Richard Burton.'

"The bartender, a black man, says, 'Who?'

" 'Richard Burton. He's one of the great actors of the world.'

"And the bartender said, 'Black or white?' "

However, if Richard desired anonymity in the town of Oroville, he was going about it in all the wrong ways. He was dating a local girl, he was out on the town at night with her, drinking and dancing and having a hell of a good time. In fact, he gifted her with a rather precious diamond ring. Diamond rings given to local girls by movie stars don't go unnoticed in Oroville, California.

One night most of the cast and crew gathered in a restaurant for a party, and of course, the locals were peering in from every available view. But Burton simply outlasted them. He was still going strong when they finally closed the place at 6 A.M. A couple of hours later he arrived on the set for his morning shooting, appearing no worse for wear, performing his scenes with complete polish.

As the shooting went on, and the friendship with the local girl flourished, the townspeople acted less and less thrilled with Richard and he with them. Once, as he and I were filming an interview outside the county courthouse, the usual crowd of gawkers gathered just a few feet away from us. I asked Richard about his stay in the town, and he began to make some rather insulting remarks about the locals, well within their earshot. "If you don't like it," one of them snapped back, "why don't you just get out!"

But he seemed to feed off the tension and turmoil, using it to stimulate his mind, to keep him sharp. Elizabeth had just arrived in town, and he became reflective.

"There was an extraordinary moment last night when I was lying in bed with—of *course*, Elizabeth—and I heard a train hooting. I said, 'Did you hear the train hooting, dear?'

"She said, 'Richard, you're drunk again.' "

I asked, "Does Elizabeth criticize you often?"

"Oh, indeed she does. Vehemently." He raised his eyes to convey his special meaning.

"And will you stand for it?"

"Oh, yes."

"For how long?"

"I suppose forever," he replied. "Very difficult to say. She is certainly dogmatic about what she thinks, about what one should do, what one should wear, what one should say. She's really very powerful in that sense. She's a kind of a latecomer to fem-lib."

His eyes glinted when he discussed Elizabeth. He was openly dating this local girl, yet clearly Elizabeth was the challenge of his life, and it was as though he dated the local girl in order to invest new drama into his relationship with Liz. She was now in town and he was prepared to deal with the fallout. It occurred to me, as Richard talked about Elizabeth, why their relationship was the favorite subject of the gossip-oriented press; the elements present were extraordinary. You had the forceful actor, considered by many critics to be among the best of his time, the conqueror now out to conquer one of the most beautiful women in the world; and you had Liz, with her penchant for dating and marrying father figures, alternately fighting with and loving them. There was marriage, divorce, remarriage and, finally, divorce. It presented a field day for amateur psychologists. As Burton and I sat, waiting for the director to call his scene, he talked about Elizabeth, then switched the subject to age and the passage of time.

"I think that when you get to the age I am (forty-eight at that point) the only present is the past, so you go back and tell stories about what somebody did when you were twelve years old, or even two and five years old. History is the past, but it's also the present," he said cryptically. "We know all the time that what's going to happen next week has already been done before, and as one gets older one becomes obsessed by the idea of history. The other day I was rereading *The Decline and Fall of the Roman Empire,* and it really is peculiarly *apt.* All the things Gibbon says about the Roman emperors—you can absolutely transfer and compare them to nowadays. You can make those emperors Nixon or Harold Wilson, Pompidou, Heath or Brezhnev, Tito. They are all exactly the same. They *cannot* change," he said with finality.

"But haven't we made some healthy advances in our time?" I was trying to follow his flow, to see where it would take us.

"What advances?"

"Scientifically. Landing men on the moon. Searching out the skies, the future."

"The least important thing that we've done, the Anglo-Saxons, shall we say," he replied, his voice heating up with the fervor of a trained Shakespearean actor, "certainly in the last hundred years, is to get a man on the moon. First of all, the idiots who went up there have no knowledge, no idea or *pur*pose. They were simply automatons. Nice men, and I wish I were as brave, but in order to be brave on that scale you have to be fairly stupid." Now the local people crowding in to eavesdrop on our interview were again annoyed. Burton was insulting the astronauts, and these people didn't like it one bit. He fed off their hostility. It motivated him.

"Unquestionably, there is no man who has gotten on the moon who really said anything of interest *whatsoever.* Neil Armstrong—he couldn't quote a poem, couldn't describe the moon, the sun, couldn't describe *anything.* 'We've made one small step' . . . I mean, come *on,* Merv. It's rubbish!"

It was obvious to me he wanted to talk about himself without actually talking about himself. Here he was, stranded in this remote town in California—he truly had no idea where in God's name he was—making a film he was only mildly interested in (he signed the contract, he told me, because he knew Lee Marvin was going to be in the picture), he was embroiled in an affair with a local girl, and Elizabeth had just arrived on the scene. He might as well have been an astronaut for all the sense he could make from what was happening. His life seemed suddenly steeped in metaphor.

As an interviewer, you have to be alert to this kind of thought pattern and follow it. If someone isn't willing to talk specifically about himself, you allow him to reveal his thoughts and personality by tracking the flow of what he *does* want to discuss.

"Then tell me, Richard, what *is* the most important advance of the last hundred years?"

"Nothing."

"Absolutely nothing?"

"Well," he waved his hand in the direction of the gathered crowd, "virtually nothing. Occasionally a man has written a verse, or said something mildly interesting, but for the most part we haven't advanced, really, for the last twenty-five hundred years."

"But you must have some heroes, people you greatly admire, men or women?"

"If I have any heroes at all, which I'm very doubtful about, I would say Socrates and Plato and Aristotle. And Alexander the Great, *maybe*. Certainly nobody since. No use talking about William Shakespeare or Dr. Johnson, because they were filthy, they smelled. Dr. Johnson had only one bath in his lifetime. I'm not sure about Shakespeare, but certainly it is true of Dr. Johnson. He used to go to a pub called the Chesterfield, and he would play and talk with a dog there, then eat with his bare hands."

I was tempted to ask him what he saw of himself in these comments, but I knew I'd lose him if I did. I'd been through this kind of interview before with Peter O'Toole, who was given to speaking in metaphors and occasional historical references.

*

SOPHIA LOREN—When I told her Richard Burton and Peter O'Toole claimed she cheats at poker:
"Who, me?"

*

OMAR SHARIF:
"Sophia loves to play poker. And she's got this thing about her that you cannot leave the table until she's winning. If it takes one week, you sit at that table; once she wins, you can get up. Usually, when you're tired, you let her win. She says, 'I've got a pair of deuces,' and you just throw your four aces out."

*

SOPHIA LOREN:
"That's not true. They are bad players. They are never able to win with me, that's why they say I cheat. Peter O'Toole still

owes me money. And O.J. Simpson owes me fifty dollars. I hate to lose."

*

SOPHIA LOREN:
"I was not born to live in a palace. I come from a poor town; I can live in a little house or I can live in a big house. It really doesn't matter, as along as I'm with my family."

*

I told Richard it was hard to imagine him growing up in a small mining village in Wales, that his spirit seemed too large for any small town.

"I never mined, myself," he quipped. "My father was a miner, most of my brothers were. I used to help out. I went down the mines at four o'clock when I finished school, I'd shovel some ground. I worked in a shop. And there was a fellow called Meredith Jones who was absolutely affronted by the fact that I was working in a *shop*. While I was polishing the brass outside the window, suddenly this strange Welshman appeared, with a bright head of red hair standing on end, and he said, 'What are you doing here? Get out. Get up. *Do* something. Go out into the world.'

"I suppose I did. Welshmen have, I think, a kind of extraordinary passion, a kind of lust for being alive, which is peculiar to us. The south of Wales, where I come from, is a kind of little America, because we have Italians, Jews, Spaniards, Negroes, Irish and Welsh, of course, all mixed. I myself am a sort of combination of many of these people. We really haven't contributed very much to the world. We have no legend of pure poetry, except for the occasional kind of freak like Dylan Thomas. We've produced no painters of any worth. My particular little nation, however, is peculiar to itself, and in fact we feel very privileged to *be* Welsh because there are so few of us."

It was time for Burton to shoot his next scene. He said to me, "To be Welsh is unique. Unique and very strange."

You don't think he could have been talking about an actor he knew, do you?

With Carroll O'Connor

With Faye Dunaway

With Carl Reiner and Wayne Rogers

With Jane Fonda

With Jack Benny and Mary Livingstone

With Lily Tomlin and Sally Field

With Omar Sharif

With Bette Davis

With Truman Capote and Cheryl Tiegs

With Carol Bayer Sager, Burt Bacharach and Christopher Cross

With Peter Ustinov and Farrah Fawcett-Majors

With Richard Burton

With Henry Fonda

With Gene Wilder

With Jack Benny

With Jane Fonda, Carole King and Gloria Steinem

With Jimmy Stewart

With George Burns

With Peter Ustinov

With Orson Welles

With Peter Fonda and Robert Blake

With Jane Fonda

With John Wayne

GENE WILDER
A Study in Shyness

THE SHYNESS OF many of the screen's most imposing actors never fails to surprise me. When you think of the millions who have seen Orson Welles, Sophia Loren, Clint Eastwood, Gene Wilder, Richard Pryor, Dustin Hoffman or dozens of other top box-office stars, and been moved with excitement, laughter or sadness by their performances, it is hard to imagine these same stars being so guarded with their personal emotions. Yet they are.

Orson Welles has gotten as far as the front door on his way to innumerable parties, yet been unable to join the festivities —his shyness supplanting his desire for a social evening. Dustin Hoffman once stood in front of my studio audience, looked them over and then couldn't look at them again for the rest of the interview. During a commercial break he said to me, "I can't describe to you how incredibly *strange* it is for me to sit here, talking about my life, and *know* I've never met these people in the audience who are listening to me, and certainly will never meet the millions of people watching at home. It is unsettling just knowing they are listening."

To overcome her shyness about appearing on my show, Sophia Loren invited me to lunch at her hotel the day before the interview. A few days before *that,* she had asked one of my talent coordinators to first prepare her for the lunch with me, and then for the show. She wanted to know what kind of questions I would ask, what kind of person I was. Over lunch we didn't discuss the upcoming interview; she simply wanted to get used to talking with me before going on national television. When she arrived at the studio Sophia was escorted to the lounge area of my dressing room, so that she wouldn't have to face the many people backstage who wanted to get a look at her. This legendary woman of the cinema sat on my couch, produced some rosary beads from her purse and recited Hail Marys to calm herself. Once we started the show she warmed up quickly, and gave the thoughtful, honest answers a shy person, once made comfortable, will usually give.

The only other guest booked on our show that evening was Burt Reynolds, who wanted to meet Sophia very badly. Now, you've all seen Burt on television, and you know that once the camera is hot so is Burt. But in the presence of Sophia he lost his voice. He just stared at her and blushed; and believe me, Burt was not acting. He was so awed by Sophia that his own deeply rooted shyness overcame him. Once Sophia leaned over impulsively and gave him a kiss, and then Burt felt a lot better about the whole situation.

*

BURT REYNOLDS:
"Unfortunately, nothing frightens me; I'm too dumb to be scared. There are a lot of things I can't handle, but nothing frightens me. I guess it was Hemingway who said that the closer you are to death the more you appreciate life. I think there's something to that."

*

Another actor who is shy to the point of preferring invisibility is Gene Wilder. In hit films like "Young Frankenstein" and

"Stir Crazy" he portrays characters with hilarious manners and quirks. But in person Gene is quiet, introspective and anything but a stand-up comedian. In fact, it's hard to imagine him even working up the nerve to get on a stage in the first place.

"What made the biggest impression on me in that regard," Gene once told me, "was my sister Coreen. I had never seen a show of any kind, and I went into a recital hall—I was eleven at the time—where Coreen was doing a piece from a play. I walked into the hall and the people in the audience were talking and laughing. All of a sudden the lights dimmed, and people started to hush. A spotlight hit the center of the stage. Out came my sister and for forty-five minutes she did her recital. I looked around the room and everyone was watching *my* sister. You could have heard a pin drop. And I thought to myself, that must be the closest thing to being God a human being can come to, that kind of power. That was the first time I was mesmerized by the power of a performer with an audience."

Like so many other performers, Gene lost a parent when he was quite young, and his ability to make people laugh was seeded during his mother's illness. He recounted the effect on him:

"My mother had a heart attack when I was six years old, and the doctor told my father, sister and me that we should try to keep mom happy and cheerful. I think if someone were reading my palm they'd look back and see a sharp curve-off right at that point of my life. I don't know what insanities take place in the minds of comic actors, comedians, of artists in general, but whatever it was stirring inside me, I got veered off toward trying to make my mother laugh. That's how I dealt with the pain I was feeling from not being able to fix her cracked heart. I was six, she had a cracked and enlarged heart, what could *I* do? So I tried to make her laugh by doing Danny Kaye routines, and then later on Sid Caesar routines. My criterion for what was really going over big—I feel a little funny about telling you this—was if she peed in her pants. If that happened, I knew the act was really going over. She would laugh so much she'd say, 'Jerry'—my real name is Jerry Silverman—'now look what you've made me do,' and she'd run off to the bathroom. I knew that meant I was on the right track. Today, when Mel Brooks and I talk about stuff for our movies, we don't want *funny*, we want 'pee in your pants' laughter."

Like Jack Benny, Gene is an actor who knows *what* makes him funny. It is not standing up in front of an audience and telling jokes. In fact, he's fairly uncomfortable with audiences. For our first interview, he asked to come into the studio during rehearsal and tape an informal conversation without an audience. This was his reasoning:

"I like the craziness to come out when I'm in front of a camera, playing a role in a movie, or on a stage, in character, *then* it can come out. But for me to talk about *myself* in front of an audience, it's not the same because they say, 'Well, he's so funny in the movies, why doesn't he get up and do some of his routines?'

"When people asked me in my youth what I wanted to be when I grew up I'd answer 'comedian.' 'Okay,' they'd say, 'let's see something funny.' But I'm not made that way. I can be funny onstage in a role with other actors. My idea of what a comedian is comes from listening to Danny Kaye albums, watching Sid Caesar in 'Your Show of Shows,' and my idea of acting comes from seeing Lee J. Cobb in 'Death of a Salesman.' I combine those elements in thinking about what I wanted to do in show business."

His ability to perform may have started with entertaining his mom, but the comedic character we identify with Gene, that of the innocent abroad, the shy fellow to whom everything happens, is patterned after his father.

"I only discovered recently," he recalls, "and to my great

surprise—I always thought everything I was doing came from my mother—that what I'm like on the screen, the kind of characters I'm playing, what my talent is *based* on, is probably ninety percent my father. The inclination to go into the arts came from my mother, but what you actually see is my father.

"My mother was studying to be a concert pianist when she married my father, who was a manufacturer of miniature bottles. He made little beer and whiskey bottles. He did this in the basement while holding down another job, then sold the bottles to novelty and souvenir shops in Milwaukee. It smelled up the basement of our building so badly that the manager had us thrown out. I was three or four years old at the time.

"My father then went into miniature chocolates, imported from Holland. The question I could never ask him, however, was why *miniature?* Why everything miniature? My father had two favorite expressions: 'Small things come in small packages' —I'm not quite sure what he meant by that—and 'Brains build boxes,' because he felt that boxes were the greatest invention of man.

"He was the most naive man, a real victim in life and the most innocent person I've ever met. I think that's what the audiences respond to in my acting. When they see me in a crazy situation in which the forces of evil are coming down on me, and they are wondering how I will get out of the mess, it's that naiveté of my father's that I call upon. Though I'm not doing it consciously, I think his effect on me is more than I'd ever dreamed it was."

Gene's own innocence caused him a certain amount of pain when at the age of thirteen he was sent to a military academy. He recalls:

"It was right here in Hollywood, and it was my first time out West. However, it turned out I was the only Jew in the academy, something I didn't understand much about. I couldn't bring myself to write home about the things that began happening. The kids would beat me up, insult me, put shoe polish on my pubic hairs, some stunt like that, every day I was there. Actually, it wasn't terrifying because I didn't understand what anti-Semitism was, and I didn't know why the boys were doing these things. I kept asking myself 'Why?' All I could figure out was that I looked a little roly-poly and pudgy. I didn't know what anyone could have against me personally."

Finding a defense for these childhood experiences sometimes develops into a career. Comedian David Brenner grew up in a tough neighborhood of South Philadelphia; he wasn't strong and rough like some of the kids, so he learned to make the others laugh, for his own protection. As a teenager I was overweight and uninterested in sports, so I wasn't going to become the campus hero by that route. I developed an ability to entertain and gained a popularity of my own. It led me into a good living.

Gene Wilder spent a lot of time thinking about how the events of his childhood shaped his present personality. He did some of his heavy thinking in rather unusual circumstances— for example, he spent two years of his military service working in a neuropsychiatric hospital. He told me how this time affected him:

"When I was with the patients I was literally locked in the ward with them. And then I realized there wasn't that much difference between what they were doing and some of the things I was *thinking*. Because of that experience, I had the courage to say, 'Maybe some of these thoughts I have are not there because God has chosen them, maybe I'm just *sick*!' So I went to see an analyst, a woman.

"She said, 'What seems to be the trouble, Gene?'

" 'I want to give away all my money.'

" 'When?'

" 'When I see crippled old people walking down the street with crutches or if I see a bloated stomach on a child—I just feel then like I should give all my money away.'

" 'Tell me, how much money do you have?'

" 'I totaled up my holdings in my head. 'Three hundred dollars, roughly.'

" 'Well, why don't you wait until you *have* some money to give away. Perhaps we'll work together before that happens, and then when you do have money maybe you'll be healthy enough and wise enough to know what to do with it.'

"That was good advice, under the circumstances. And I realized that I had an inability to express anger and sexual aggression, which I rerouted into obsessional thinking about ethical, moral and religious thoughts. I was going through a period of struggle, trying to turn from Jerry Silverman into Gene Wilder."

I've often wondered if too much self-analysis could prove fatal to a comic actor. Might they become normal and lose their ability to be funny?

"Baloney," Gene says. "Freud was asked the same question. His answer was that whereas it's true that a person with a little bit of talent, after analysis, might decide to give it all up, the person with a *lot* of talent would probably use that talent more freely. And for the one who gave it all up because of analysis, the world would probably be better off without his talent, simply because it wouldn't have been very big.

"I feel that after analysis I was able to write, and without it I don't think I would *ever* have gone into directing. When you are directing, you are God, you're all powerful and you have complete control.

"This is the real conversion I had to make going from acting to directing. It is not in the responsibility you have for technical things, but rather in changing roles from the son to the father. All actors—whether in a play or a movie—are reaching out to the director all the time. They say, 'Did I do good? Encourage me, love me, tell me I was okay.' The director, regardless of whether he is a man or woman, automatically becomes a father figure. The actors are looking to you for feedback. 'How well did I deliver that line? Was I good?' I don't think I could ever have accepted that role without analysis. And the desire to direct came after my desire to write. Mel Brooks told me that once you've written for films you'll want to direct just to protect your scripts. So you do it all—act, write and direct—and as Mel says, 'You do it all and either you fall on your ass or you're gonna be all right and they'll let you try it again.' "

Gene has now reached that rare plateau in Hollywood that enables him to choose where, when and under what circumstances he will work. The option to write, act and direct is his. And his standing as a box-office attraction is such that he will make several million dollars from each successful film. He takes it all well in stride.

In the summer of 1979 we took "The Merv Griffin Show," along with a planeload of celebrities, to Venice, Italy, for a tennis tournament. Mel Brooks, Anne Bancroft, Gene Wilder, Carl Reiner, Penny Marshall, Rob Reiner, Connie Stevens, Dyan Cannon and many other stars were along for the week. But it was Gene who seemed to fascinate my staff, simply because he is so pleasantly mysterious. I'm told the staff would daily compare their "Wilder" sightings. While the other celebrities were busy playing tennis or enjoying lavish parties, Gene was spotted frequenting offbeat art galleries or looking for a highly recommended local restaurant. When it was time to tape an interview with him, he was partial to doing it in the hotel's kitchen and wine cellar, where he could examine their library of rare vintages, rather than by the tennis courts with all the tourists watching. What this indicates to me is that Gene is someone who will have a long and successful career, because he is aware of what makes him comfortable and what makes him creative, and he follows this self-knowledge rather than trying to live up to somebody else's image of a movie star.

"It's the amazing thing about all performing artists," he told me. "We say all the time how nervous and shy we are as people, while the other half of us is saying, 'Look at *me*, want *me*, don't look at him or her, just *me!*' And that is a dichotomy that's often difficult to understand."

HENRY, JANE AND PETER FONDA

An American Drama

I'M SURE THAT before this decade is over we'll be seeing a television mini-series "docudrama" called simply, "The Fondas." For theirs is a story of brilliant careers, powerful personalities and dramatic private lives; it is a mix of elements that Hollywood producers pray for.

Henry Fonda appeared on my show many times; he was a private man, not given to discussing his personal life on national television. Ask him questions about the theater and he'd talk your ear off, but the rest of his life he left alone. Only persistence on the part of writer Howard Teichman pushed Fonda to consent to an authorized biography. But in the beginning, Teichman told me, Fonda was dead-set against the idea. "No way I want to do a biography," Henry told Teichman. "Too much pain connected with my life. Too many suicides, too many marriages I'm ashamed of." Hank Fonda always seemed to feel that his work, such as "Mr. Roberts," "The Grapes of Wrath" and, finally, "On Golden Pond," was all the public needed to know about him.

When the Teichman biography was published, a year prior to Henry's death, I invited the author and Peter Fonda to discuss the book and the man.

"I must say," Peter Fonda told me, "I wish I'd read the book

73

forty-one years ago. I would have understood so much more about him as a person, instead of taking his silences, and the way he is as a person, against *myself*, taking it personally. I would have understood where he was coming from and not had such a troubled attitude about him. As a father he was totally cut off. He was a clam. He didn't know how to carry on a conversation, didn't feel comfortable, at least that's what he claims. When he has a story to tell, though, he tells it quite well. You see, he doesn't feel comfortable with conversational routines, he didn't know how to say simple things. He was afraid, and I now know why, to say things like 'I love you.' Several years ago, I said to myself, this is enough of this, and I told him, come on, let's finish it up and say 'I love you,' and I sort of trained him. I don't mean to be funny about it, because it wasn't funny and he was quite serious, but I started training him on the phone. I'd say, 'I love you, Dad,' and the phone gave him a bit of distance. The first time he said it was 'Iloveyouson,' and then he hung up. We progressed to 'I love you, Dad' and 'Iloveyou*too*son,' and then he gradually was able to beat me to the punch, and finally he was able to look me in the eyes and say it to me. Well, that was very important. He might have passed without being able to say that to me, or to Jane or Amy or his grandchildren.

"It's not that he isn't a loving person at all. He just has no character with a script that says 'Henry Fonda says, 'I love you, son.' If he had that he'd be able to handle it. He has to have the mask in order to express. The film 'On Golden Pond' is about him, even though the writer didn't have him in mind when it was conceived. It was great Jane got to do 'it' with Dad. She had never been able to express herself with him the way she wanted. I mean, I look at my own children, they can come up and grab me and say they love me, hang all over me, and that's fabulous to have. That's what really got me thinking I'd better get my act together and let Henry know I love him, verbally. I've written it to him in letters and I've told him this, but it's never been literal, touching each other. And I feel sad about that."

I told Peter about the time I was at San Francisco airport, putting my son on a plane; he was seventeen or eighteen, and six feet tall. As he said goodbye he gave me a hug and went off to catch his flight. As I stood there watching him board the plane a man came up to me and said, "I watched you say goodbye to your son; is he always affectionate like that?" I told him yes. And the man looked sad and said, "Do you know what I would give if just one of my sons ever did that to me?" And I said, "Why wait? Do it to them first."

"Right," Peter Fonda replied, "that's the answer I came to with Henry."

Howard Teichman nodded agreement. "I think Peter hit it on the nose. I can just tell you from my conversations with Henry that he thinks Greta Garbo is a *big* talker. He is a cold, warm, very tough, very soft, very human person. As Peter said, as long as Henry has the mask to put on, has the dialogue given him by the playwright or screenwriter, he's okay. No anxieties, no fears, no problems. But once he walks off that stage, or that set, he becomes a very internal, withdrawn man, and it's hard to break through that wall of silence. He's very proud, but also ashamed. Ashamed that he had five wives. He doesn't seem like the kind of man to *have* five wives. He couldn't believe it himself."

"The real tragedy," Peter Fonda added, "was his first love. His first marriage broke his heart so badly when it dissipated that he never recovered, until he met Shirley [his widow]. He simply never recovered, he withdrew totally from everybody."

"We had a hard time talking about Margaret Sullavan, his first wife," Howard Teichman said. "They were married about three months when one day Henry was standing in line for a casting call, and he heard two actors say, 'You know that

Margaret Sullavan is having an affair with Jed Harris [the producer].' " And that just wiped Henry out then and there. He couldn't trust a woman from then on."

It is interesting to speculate on how Henry Fonda's distance as a father might have led his daughter Jane to make such a conspicuous and spectacular success of her life. Peter Fonda told me that the scene in "On Golden Pond" where Jane literally does back flips into the lake to impress her father mirrors the relationship between them in real life. Evidently, Henry Fonda did not lavish attention on Jane when she was growing up, and the "back flips" she did to catch his eye became increasingly important. As an actress she has worked herself into the prime position of her generation; there *is* no actress more respected or more in demand than Jane Fonda. She has made use of this professional success to produce and participate in such films as "Coming Home," "The China Syndrome" and "On Golden Pond," that she feels both entertain and make important social statements. She is unafraid of risking fame and fortune to speak out on issues that in her opinion transcend the protection of her public image.

Some of Jane's critics suggest she was a sex kitten young actress who in the late sixties jumped on the anti-war bandwagon when it became fashionable to do so, and that her marriages to Roger Vadim, the director, and to Tom Hayden, the political activist, reflect a search for a male image who appreciates her most valued qualities: Vadim, the actress; and Hayden, her social conscience. But Jane has always shown an admirable lack of interest in her critics and, if anything, I think, people haven't given her *enough* credit for what she's accomplished.

I first interviewed her back in the mid-sixties, when she was married to the French film director Roger Vadim. Even then

Jane was anything but an empty-headed actress, as some critics have suggested. She was intelligent, definite and an equal partner with Vadim in the marriage. Perhaps the fact that Vadim had been with Brigitte Bardot prior to Jane left the door open to the sex kitten image. I remember one of my first conversations with Fonda and Vadim; I asked him why he was such a successful director of women (he was responsible for making Bardot a star in America).

"What is important," he said, "is to take from an actress on the screen what her talent gives you and to try and hide what is weak on her. To get a lot of things out of a woman you must pretend to understand everything and to be very cool, and little by little you get what you want. I think that for the theater, not in life. When you hold too strongly a woman you lose her. So in one sense I become a slave to women."

Jane looked at her husband, shook her head, then spoke up. "I don't see why you say 'slave.' You said you *pretend* to be cool and to understand a woman. But I think you *are* cool and you *do* understand. You are not a slave."

Vadim considered his wife's comment, then continued. "You must help people to be themselves, and to help people to be themselves you must make them comfortable. It is not always holding them too strong. Don't ask someone always to do exactly what you want them to do. I wait for what a woman gives me. In a way I meet them in their own garden, and I am feminine to win."

I looked puzzled, so Jane explained: "He becomes feminine in order to get what he wants. I know what he means. He is right."

Vadim met Jane on her own turf, "in her own garden," which perhaps was something she had not experienced with her father. And out of that marriage the strength to assert herself increased. He caused her to search her own limits. She said of Vadim as director: "First of all, he says he makes the actress feel comfortable. I don't agree with that, and I think that's *why* he is a good director. He always keeps you off balance. Actresses and actors are usually quite stupid about what we think we can do well, and it is the director who comes along and makes us use muscles we have never used before, just tips us over a little bit to get good results. Vadim does that all the time. I'll say, 'I can't do that, I can't play that scene,' and he'd make me do it, and it would turn into a good scene." Judging by the changes that occurred in Jane's life in the sixties, her years with Vadim brought about a personal expansion, as well as her growth as an actress. That first interview was in 1967. The next version of Jane Fonda I saw was one of an even more strong-willed woman, this time with a political consciousness.

Living in France with Vadim gave her a perspective on this country she might never have had if she'd remained in Hollywood. She remembers those times well. "I guess I was brought up like most people; our country could do no wrong. I had been in France during the Eisenhower administration, the Kennedy administration, and was living there in 1968 with Vadim. I watched the respect for our country go downhill, and I didn't really pay too much attention, because I didn't understand what it meant.

"A Frenchman came up to me one day and said, 'Well, how do you think your country is doing now?' The papers had just reported that famous incident where we had bombed a Vietnamese village in order to 'save' it. I became very defensive. At the same time, there was the anti-war movement going on in America, and I could watch French television and see hundreds of thousands of Americans protesting the war. It made me think that something was going on that I didn't understand. So I began to study and to read. When I began to learn what was going on in Vietnam, I couldn't believe it. I started talking with soldiers who had been in Vietnam, and my reaction to what they told me was one of anger; I felt that I had been deceived and manipulated by a lot of government propaganda. I wasn't a young student anymore, I was thirty-two years old. And I said, 'Okay, half of my life is already over and I want to go back to the United States and participate with other people to expose what is going on.'

"I remember my business manager and my public relations people saying, 'Oh, Jane, don't do that. You're going to ruin your career!' But I thought to myself, What has my career meant to me at this point? Am I all that happy with my career? I've lived in Hollywood long enough to know that all the mansions and swimming pools also mean psychiatrists; it means having your children alienated from you; it means not necessarily a great deal of happiness. I felt that I had spent enough time being cynical and irrelevant and apathetic. I came along in the anti-war movement when it was relatively fashionable to be against the war. But all those before me sort of helped me understand that there may be a lot wrong with the government, but there's nothing wrong with the American people."

Despite what Jane says about her career in the late sixties, her move into political reform wasn't all that easy. She knew that by speaking out against the government she was going to alienate a large part of the American public, all those people between New York and Los Angeles who go to the movies and make million-dollar salaries for actors and actresses possible. Her abilities as an actress were what gave her a public platform, and by taking an anti-Nixon, anti-war stand in 1968, she risked losing that platform forever.

"I had to assume that I would not work again," she told me. "I had to make a choice about whether I would stop being a political activist against the war or worry about acting; I didn't think I could live with myself if I didn't do what I felt needed to be done."

Jane not only risked her career; she risked something that was less tangible and more precious to her: her relationship with her father. Peter Fonda recalled to me a moment when Henry Fonda realized his children were taking a controversial stand. "He once made a comment to me about the 'peaceniks' making the war last longer than it had to" (a theory supported by no less a source than Henry Kissinger, and discussed later in this book). "I said to my dad, 'I'm one of those people that you're talking about.' We had a tremendous locking of horns, as it were, that left Henry in tears. I felt very bad about that, but I knew I was right in what I was saying. But we never stopped talking, we never got to the point of, 'Unless you apologize we're never to speak again.' "

Howard Teichman pointed out to me, however, that Jane felt the terrible pressure of her anti-war stand potentially separating her from her father. Teichman reports that at one point Henry said to Jane, "If I find out you're a Communist or a Communist sympathizer, I, your father, will be the first one to turn you in, because I fought for this country, and I love it. Everything isn't perfect here, but it's a lot better here than it is elsewhere." But to Henry Fonda's credit, Teichman says, he allowed his children to educate him. "He was not opposed to their activism. He let them go, and they showed him the light."

Jane later recalled for me the poignant moment when she arranged a screening of "Coming Home" for her father. That was the film, produced by Jane's company, starring her and Jon Voight, about the effect of the Vietnam war on men who fought it, particularly the men who returned from the war crippled for life. After Henry saw the film, Jane remembers, he couldn't talk for hours, he was so shook up and moved by it.

I had the same reaction. We had agreed to salute the cast of the film—Jane, Voight and Bruce Dern. On the morning of our afternoon taping I went to a screening of the film with several of my staff. When the film ended no one in the screening room spoke. We all looked at each other but no one could say anything after the impact of the film. During the taping that afternoon I was very subdued. Jane Fonda had learned how to present her concerns in a way that carried a thousand times the emotional weight of any speech or debate.

Instead of backing down from "the system," she is assaulting it head on. In the early seventies she was obviously considered a "security risk" by certain people in the government, and she became a target of FBI surveillance.

"J. Edgar Hoover wrote a letter to the FBI office in Los Angeles," Jane asserts, "asking *them* to write a letter, from a non-existent person, to Army Archerd, the Hollwood columnist. This person said in the letter that they had seen me at a fund-raising gathering, raising money to buy guns, and leading to a chat where I used foul language and suggested that Richard Nixon should be killed. Totally fabricated, needless to say, and at the bottom of the memo, J. Edgar Hoover wrote, 'This will serve to discredit her in Hollywood.' In other words, it was a carefully orchestrated plan to create the impression that I was violence-prone, foul-mouthed and generally had that kind of attitude. . . . The FBI went to the bank in New York, and without a subpoena, illegally took from that bank every financial record in my name, every check stub, *everything*. It was a flagrant violation of my constitutional rights, and they pulled out the old bugaboo, 'She's a national security risk.' I'd never even broken the law, never was guilty of a misdemeanor, but I was a national security risk.

"The most frightening thing of all happened in 1973. The FBI sent a woman undercover agent, disguised as a reporter, who was interested in my activities as an actress and political activist. But her real purpose in coming to my house was to find out when my child was to be born. *Why?* Why did they need to know when my child was going to be born? It is so strange."

And now Jane is working within the system that tried to

subvert her, by supporting the political campaigns of her husband Tom Hayden. During his campaign for the California House of Representatives, she walked door to door in her district, talking with people about her husband's and her beliefs. She has avoided raising her children in the opulence of Beverly Hills or Bel Air, though she could well afford to. She and Tom live in a modest home in Santa Monica. Her children are, of course, a major part of her daily schedule.

Jane Fonda has done what so few people are able to do: understand what they did not like in their own childhood and not compound the error with their own children.

And it is to her credit that she values that accomplishment above the Oscars and everything else she's attained.

JOSH LOGAN
The Great Raconteur

I LEARNED MORE about Henry Fonda, the man, from talking with Peter and Jane and Howard Teichman than I ever did through interviewing Henry. But he was always willing to talk shop, particularly when in the company of friends, such as Josh Logan and Jimmy Stewart. All three went to Princeton together, shared an apartment in New York and collectively gave America some of its greatest moments of popular entertainment.

As a director, writer and producer Josh Logan brought to the stage such triumphs as *Mister Roberts, Morning's at Seven, Charley's Aunt, South Pacific, Picnic, Fanny* and the film versions of several of those classics. Josh is one of show business's greatest raconteurs and memoirists. During one of our visits together, he recalled his first encounter with Henry Fonda, a meeting that eventually led, down a twisting path, to their collaboration on the unforgettable *Mister Roberts*.

"I was nineteen and a member of the University Players at Princeton," Josh remembered. "I was playing the character of Huckley in George Kelly's play *The Torchbearers*; it's a very funny play about amateur theatricals. Imitating something I'd seen on a stage once, I played the character with a very flat voice. During our second night, as soon as I opened my mouth, there was the most tremendous noise that came from someone in the audience. It was kind of a strangulated sob; it was high, and had nothing to do with humor or mirth; it was like somebody crying off-key, a stretched-out, strange sound that was such a shock to the rest of the audience that they all laughed. Well, I was dying to get a laugh, so I was delighted; I hadn't done very well the night before. But this night every time I opened my mouth I was met by this sound from the audience, *whatever* it was. I began to love this man, whoever it was who was laughing, because he made me a star that night.

"In the dressing room afterwards a friend of mine, Bernie Hannigan from Omaha, arrived and said, 'Fellas, I'd like you to meet another friend of mine from Omaha, Henry Fonda.' This tall, skinny guy walked in with his chin way back, his pelvis way forward, his chest held in; he was wearing black golf socks, skinny white knickers and a white pullover sweater. He looked rather shy and worried. He said to me, 'Were you Huckley?' I said yes. And out came this laugh, and he fell on the floor. Well, of course, I loved him and I always will."

Henry Fonda validated the story, but added an explanation for the strange quality of his laugh that night. "Bernie Hannigan and I decided at the last minute to go down and see the University Players, so the only seats that we could get were singles. I got a seat with dowagers on both sides. I didn't know anything about the play, so when I heard that voice come out of Josh, and I didn't know what his character was about, I collapsed and I had to try and strangle my laugh because of those dowagers I was with. But I couldn't control it."

"We became great pals after that," Josh Logan continued. "We even put an act together. We had taken over this theater connected to a tearoom—it was really a nightclub. And we had to run it, even though we were breaking our tails to run the theater. Fonda and I once went out to do the nightclub show without any preparation whatsoever. I played that same voice I did with the Huckley character, because I knew it made Henry laugh, and he played Little Elmer, an idiot kid who did imitations of fish and birds. It was the craziest act you ever saw, but the audience just howled. Fonda was so excited playing those little birds and all, and I was getting jealous because he was upstaging me. So I picked up a hundred-pound block of ice, put it in his arms and all he could do was stand there holding it. That was the end of our sketch."

From this modest beginning, however, came a friendship that brought us one of Fonda's most famous roles.

"I came East with a script of John O'Hara's *Appointment in Samarra,*" Henry told me. "I'd wanted to do this story in a film for years, but the script didn't turn out well, and I figured Josh Logan was the only person I knew who could fix it. I brought the script to New York to see if he could find out what its problems were. But he wouldn't listen to me, because he had just finished writing, with Tom Heggen, a play called *Mister Roberts,* and he practically grabbed me, sat me down and read the play aloud.

"At the end of the reading I laughed, cried and everything else. I remember getting up and calling my agent in California. I said to him, 'You've got to get me out of that film I'm supposed to be starting in two weeks, because I've just heard the most wonderful play, and I've got to do it.' He did get me out of the film and soon I was back in New York rehearsing *Mister Roberts.*"

Josh Logan added to the story: "The strange thing was when Tom and I were writing we were also casting in our minds. When we finished I said to Tom, 'Who do you think should play Roberts? It should be a big, tall, romantic guy . . . ' And Tom said, 'You know whom I have had in mind all along is Henry Fonda.' And I said, 'Good God, that's what *I've* been thinking.' We hadn't said it to each other only because each was afraid the other would turn it down."

That Henry Fonda would turn down a big-money film deal to take a stage role that could end in one night is, at the very least, interesting. But he told me that the theater had always been his first love. "The theater is indulgence for me, because in films you act for one or two minutes, then stop. The scenes you do are unrelated in sequence; it takes months of editing to piece all the scenes together. You never play the part from beginning to end, so you don't have the feeling you created the role. On the other hand, in the theater you rehearse extensively and then open the play when it is ready. The curtain goes up, you start and go straight through, beginning to end. In film you do a scene, go to lunch while the film goes to the lab, and you might never see it again."

No actor—other than perhaps Brando in *A Streetcar Named Desire*—has been more praised for his work on stage than Henry Fonda in *Mister Roberts*. Once that kind of praise is lavished on an actor for the portrayal of a role, many of them forget the contributions of the writer and director. But not Henry Fonda. When I asked him about Josh's contributions to the development of the Roberts character, Henry remembered one particular evening when the role was brought fully into focus.

"I remember being at a point in the development of the character in rehearsals in which I was still reaching and wondering, not sure of things. At the time Josh and I were both staying in the same hotel. One day after rehearsals Josh told me to come up to his room for a talk. His wife had already gone to bed. Josh began to talk about the character of Roberts. I may be exaggerating, but it was an hour or two later that I was still sitting there listening; I hadn't moved or opened my mouth, while Josh talked and paced at the same time. I get emotional just thinking about that night. He paced and talked about Roberts, and I just ate every word up. *There's* a director who knows *how* to communicate with an actor."

Curiously, when Henry Fonda thought back on *Mister Roberts,* it was not the opening night that brought forth his favorite memory; rather it was the evening when the cast first previewed the show for some friends. "The high point for me was when we first did a run-through. For those who don't know what a run-through is, I will explain. Up to a certain point in the rehearsal of a play, the director starts and stops the scenes, doing a single scene over and over, polishing it. Eventually, with us it was about the third week, and the play was ready to go all the way through. But no costumes, sets, props, nothing; a bare stage in a theater.

"Josh had arranged for about a hundred friends to come to the Belasco Theater on a Sunday afternoon to watch this first run-through. We started at the beginning and went through without stopping, and it was the first time that I, or any of the other actors, realized the cumulative effect the play had, the building of emotion upon emotion. We had no curtain, so when the play was over the actors stood in the wings looking out at the audience. They were applauding. Somebody turned to us, because the people out there wouldn't stop applauding, and said we should take a bow. Finally, we straggled out there in a small mob to take a bow."

Josh Logan adds: "Henry actually left the theater after taking his first bow; he walked up the block. Somebody called to him and said, 'They're still in there applauding, Mr. Fonda.' The cast returned and the applause built up again. You *do* see something raw in run-throughs that you can't see when the makeup and lights are on. Sometimes costumes and scenery can hurt a play; I've had that happen many times— the run-through was more powerful than the play."

History proved that *Mister Roberts* was as powerful in its final production as in the run-through. The opening night audience was every bit as responsive as those first viewers. "They wouldn't stop applauding," Fonda remembered. "I couldn't see because the lights were in my eyes, but I was told Noel Coward got up and stood on his seat. And it just got to be more and more and more. I didn't know what to do. Finally, I put up my hands to stop the applause and said, 'That's all they *wrote*, but we can start again!' "

Henry Fonda was not the only actor Josh Logan nurtured and encouraged at Princeton; there were many others, most notably a tall, skinny youth by the name of Jimmy Stewart. I've always admired Stewart's acting because he is a master of underplay; his roles fit him like a well-tailored suit, and he never seems to be straining. When he appeared on my show with his lifelong friend, Josh Logan, Jimmy Stewart described his move into acting as more accident than intention.

"I was a cheerleader, and not the best. I started out in school to be an engineer, and a fella came up to me, during my sophomore year, and explained that in order to be an engineer, 'You have to know a little bit about mathematics . . . you know *nothing* about mathematics." He advised me to change majors before they threw me out. I got into architecture, which I like very much. I planned to continue into graduate school, but Josh Logan asked me to join the University Players, and this invitation changed the whole thing. He is responsible for getting me into the acting racket. And I just thought the whole thing was fun; I enjoyed it. Christmas vacation, we got to go on a trip around the country, and the alumni would invite us to their homes. It was always great fun. How any of us got through exams, I don't know."

In the days when Henry Fonda and Jimmy Stewart were starting their acting careers, the profession was considered frivolous by "serious" folks, so I asked Jimmy if it required especially understanding parents to support his intentions.

"As I remember, my father reached for a chair and sat down when I broke the news it was acting rather than architecture. But both my parents, bless their hearts, said, 'If that's what you want to do, go ahead and give it a try.' My father was a hardware merchant; his store was old-fashioned and very special. He kept it in operation until the year before his death at age eighty-nine. I think the reason he kept it going that long was because he was sure they were eventually going to catch up with me out in Hollywood, and then I'd have something to come back to."

When Jimmy Stewart, Henry Fonda and Josh Logan left school, they went to New York and rented an apartment together. It was the sort of day-to-day, happy-go-lucky existence you'd expect from a bunch of young actors. Stewart remembers those days fondly. "We got the apartment cheap, and nobody could understand why it was so cheap. Later we learned that our building was owned by Legs Diamond, the gangster. He had his headquarters next to us; we always thought that they were just a bunch of unusually interesting characters. There were usually five or six of us in our apartment, depending on who was out of work. At any given time, one or two guys usually had jobs, and whoever had money would buy food for the rest. We all kept working in the theater, and I remember the excitement because although it was the absolute dead bottom of the depression, the New York theater was very active. It was tremendously exciting to all of us."

One source of their excitement, Henry Fonda told me, was their neighbor, Miss Greta Garbo. There was no fence separating the backyards of the two buildings, and Miss Garbo decided the presence of the young actors was more than she could bear. So she built a seven-foot wall. Fonda, Stewart and Logan thought it would be amusing to tunnel under the wall and surprise the actress. But in doing so they hit a water main that completely flooded *both* yards.

Josh Logan not only spotted in Henry Fonda and Jimmy Stewart an innate talent that the world later applauded; he also worked with some of the cinema's great leading ladies, notably Marilyn Monroe and Marlene Dietrich. It is never fair to ask Josh to name his favorite actor, but I did ask him about actresses, and his answer came without hesitation.

"I think I directed the most talented actress of all, as well as the most beautiful," he said. "Marilyn Monroe. I think her greatest performance was 'Bus Stop,' no question about it. In the first place, it's the best part she ever had written for her. I think I treated her well, encouraged and helped her; she had a great cast around her, and all those reasons are why the picture turned out to be so good.

"Working with her was a very touching experience. She had never had any education; as a kid she'd been kicked around from one home to another; she never studied, never read, she didn't know anything about the intellectual world. And when I worked with her, for the first time in her life, when she was thirty years old, she was discovering the intellect. Her joy in learning about Freud, Einstein and Stanislavsky was marvelous to witness. People always referred to her as the *dumb* blonde. It wasn't true. She was just an *uneducated* blonde. But a gorgeous one, who was sensitive and funny.

*

OMAR SHARIF—On leading ladies:
"I think this is perhaps very unprofessional to say, but I find

it impossible if I work for eight or nine hours a day playing love scenes with a girl, seeing her every day for three months . . . I find it impossible when they say 'cut' to turn it off like that. Something lingers on. With Barbra Streisand on 'Funny Girl' it was different because I was in love with her, I really was. And it was one-sided, yet I did love her a lot. She had a lot of affection for me, but it just didn't go beyond that."

*

"I remember an incident that showed her excitement about learning. She had studied with Lee Strasberg, the great acting teacher, and learned about Stanislavsky and Freud, and now she was beginning to apply it. Every time she discovered something she tried to tell poor Don Murray, another actor in the film, about her discovery. He'd nod and say, 'I know, I know, I *know.*' He just wanted to be left alone to study his lines. So now comes the scene in 'Bus Stop' when Marilyn is in bed in a boarding house and Don comes rushing in and says, 'Wake up, Cherry! The sun's out. No wonder you're so pale and white.' We shot the scene, then we tried it once again, because something had gone wrong. We did it again, but Don says, 'Wake up, Cherry! The sun's out. No wonder you're so pale and scaly.'

"I said, 'Sorry, cut; you said "scaly" instead of "white," Don.'

"He replied, 'I said scaly instead of white? I couldn't have. Why would I say scaly?'

"Don sat on one end of Marilyn's bed and I sat on the other, while we waited for them to reload the camera to reshoot the scene. Marilyn is sitting quietly under the covers. Suddenly her voice popped out from the top of the bed:

" 'Don,' she said, 'do you realize what you did? You made a Freudian slip.'

"He said, '*What?*'

"Marilyn replied, 'A Freudian slip. It means you were in the mood of the scene. Unconsciously you were playing the scene correctly, because it is a sexual scene, Don, and let's face it, you had that kind of thought.'

"He looked at Marilyn with exasperation. 'I don't know what the *hell* you're talking about.'

" 'Don't you see,' she answered, 'you said "scaly" instead of "white," which means unconsciously you were thinking of a snake. A snake is a phallic symbol, Don,' Marilyn said proudly, then asked him: 'Do you know what a phallic symbol *is*, Don?'

" 'Know what it is?' he said to her, throwing back his hands. 'I've *got* one!.' "

*

OMAR SHARIF:
"I think the woman changes all the time, is in constant evolution; she's very complex, very complicated, whereas the man, I feel, is the same throughout the ages, he hasn't changed at all. We have the same rather childish mentality. Men are very square, very linear, not at all very complex . . . We're really children, and I think women actually like that side of our nature; the mixture of strong and weak is very attractive to women. They like the strong side, because that's the side that is going to be protective, manly; but they also need to find in a man a lot of weak spots that they can mother."

*

Walt Disney once said that there are no great men who did not, at certain points in their careers, experience colossal failures. Certainly everyone who has been even moderately successful in show business will attest to that. It is a question I like to ask successful people, for often we reveal more about ourselves when discussing our failures than we do in recounting successes. Josh Logan recalls his major disaster—the

Broadway musical *Mr. President.*

"*Mr. President* was the biggest bomb of 1962. Irving Berlin had written the music, so he had a bomb right along with me. It was a big musical comedy about a president, and everybody thought it was going to be a smash. In fact, we sold two million dollars' worth of tickets in advance. However, it was absolutely despised by the critics when it opened in Boston.

"Still, it received world-wide talk because people thought for some reason it was a takeoff on the Kennedys, simply because it was called *Mr. President.* It wasn't about the Kennedys; it was just a corny old story about an old President. Maybe it was about Harry Truman, who knows. Anyway, it received terrible notices. Immediately after those awful reviews came out we had to go to Washington, D.C., to do the show as a benefit for the Kennedy Foundation. Ethel Kennedy was in charge of it, so all the Kennedys were going to be there, even Jack and Jackie. I thought to myself, 'I know it's going to be awful, but I'll just sit out front and watch the bloody thing . . . '

"During the evening people looked up at the box where President Kennedy was supposed to be sitting, but only Jackie was there; the President had been delayed by a crisis, something to do with Cuba. He didn't arrive until the second act.

"Now, I should preface this by pointing out that when you have trouble in a play, and you're running the show out of town, you're sure to find somebody who can fix it up. Some friend of a friend will suggest, 'Why don't you cut the girl out of that part in the second act, put her in the third act and you'll have a hit.' Then somebody else will suggest cutting out all the music and replacing it with zither players—that kind of thing. Somebody even told me to throw out the captain in *Mister Roberts.*

"So there we were watching *Mr. President,* and it was a *bomb,* and there was nothing to do to save it. I decided that I'd have a good time despite it. Later there was a big party at the British embassy, and all the Kennedys were there. I looked around for a vacant seat and found myself next to Alice Longworth, Teddy Roosevelt's daughter, a brilliant, wise old lady. She had no idea who I was, but she was very charming and asked me to sit with her. The next thing she said was, 'Did you see that terrible show we all saw tonight?'

" 'Yes, I'm afraid I did.'

"Then she said, 'You know, *this* one,' pointing across the table at one of the writers of *Mr. President,* 'he thinks it's good.' She just laughed.

"All of a sudden I saw someone at the other side of the table signaling me to turn around. And right there in my face was the President of the United States, Jack Kennedy. He was looking at me, and *I* didn't know what to do. I felt guilty, then I thought, 'What have I done? The show, that's all, I shouldn't feel like a defendant.' Surely, he didn't want to talk to me about the *show.* He said, 'Are you the director?'

" 'Yes, sir.'

"Then he said, 'You know in the show where the President lands in Moscow? I think it would be much better if the President landed in Copenhagen, which is in a neutral country, and in that way you can get the message across better.'

"I just stared at him without answering, because the thought was running through my mind: 'I've been through shows since I was nineteen years old and they've been fixed by people I'd meet in the hotel lobby, but this is the first time a musical comedy is being fixed by a President of the United States!' "

JACK PAAR
The Human Factor on TV

THE TALK SHOW, which has undergone a countless variety of
forms and presentations since its inception in the fifties, is at
its entertaining best when the viewer is seeing a "real" moment; that is, an unrehearsed remark, gesture or reaction by a
guest or host that leaves the audience feeling they've witnessed
a genuine emotion. Television viewers are used to seeing people perform, act and project personalities that at home seem
practiced and polished. So when one of those "real" moments
happens, it's remembered and discussed the next day. I'll give
you a few examples.

When I interviewed Gerald Ford after he left the Presidency, the first portion of our talk was fairly predictable. He
discussed the campaign, his term in office, and his projections
for the new Carter administration. It was a friendly, informative conversation, but businesslike. When we began discussing
his firm belief in allowing Vietnamese refugees to seek shelter
in America, it led to Mr. Ford talking about his own childhood,
and of how he learned one day at the age of twelve that the
man he believed to be his father wasn't. His voice fell from the
hefty timbre of politics to a soft, emotional tone. The former
President's eyes were a bit cloudy when he then told me the
story of the day his real father came to the diner where young

Gerald Ford worked and introduced himself. They talked, Ford's father gave his son twenty-five dollars, then disappeared from his son's life once again.

On another show, the legendary heart surgeon Dr. Christiaan Barnard told us a sad and personal story about his son. As he contemplated what he was saying, his eyes filled with tears and he began sobbing. We stopped the show until he recovered.

Moments like these give a talk show a sense of immediacy and reality. And I think there is one man responsible for introducing this human element into television: Jack Paar.

Anyone who has hosted a talk show admires and is indebted to Steve Allen for his contributions to "The Tonight Show." But I think my own style developed from years of watching Paar. Jack gave television a sense of detail. He let us in on the funny nuances of life as he told stories about himself, his family, as he observed the goings-on in the world. He let the audience in on his opinions and emotions, without ever losing sight of humor. And his honest reactions catapulted him into the position of being television's hottest host. The papers were always writing about something that Paar did last night on his show, whether it was walking out on his network because executives had censored a harmless joke, or creating an international incident during his visit to the Berlin Wall. Jack introduced "real" moments to talk shows, and it was a big disappointment to a lot of us when he left the public eye. I invited him many times to appear as a guest on my show, and it took the bait of a luxurious trip to Monte Carlo for a tennis tournament to coax Jack finally out of hiding.

We took a planeload of celebrities in June 1977 to play some tennis and do a few television shows, and I was looking forward to sitting down with Jack for a good chat.

Even though we had him halfway around the world in the tiny principality of Monaco, Jack still proved elusive. The trip consisted of a three-day tennis tournament and a series of lavish parties and social events, all covered by our cameras. But each time we tried to grab Jack for an interview he was just leaving for lunch, a shopping trip or was off to play tennis. And in the true Paar style, he kept popping up when we least expected it.

One morning I was doing an interview with the Dick Van Patten family on the terrace of the Hôtel du Paris, and in the middle of the interview Jack Paar's elfish face poked through a hedge and he said, "Merv, I just wanted to tell you Miriam and I are off for a drive and we can't do an interview now." Then at one of the black-tie functions we tried to corner Jack, but he breezed by, saying, "I'll be back as soon as I have this damned tuxedo pressed!" He was gone again. He'd found a way to make himself the unstated theme of our three shows—The Search For Jack Paar—without having to do anything at all!

Finally, one of our tennis matches was interrupted by a violent rainstorm, and I caught Jack in the restaurant of the tennis club, toweling off.

Immediately, I asked him how he could live in the quiet Connecticut countryside and still contain all the energy and humor I'd seen him exhibiting the last few days.

"This is happening because I've not been around people in a very long time," he said. "That sounds like a setup, but I mean it. When I get around show business and actors again then I remember what I once was. For years I've been a very quiet person; six months will go by in my rural community and nobody recognizes me or mentions anything about show business."

Paar brought an unusual talent to television. Although he had acted, he didn't consider himself an actor and he certainly wasn't a singer or nightclub comedian. I asked him how he developed his style as a host.

"It's all I could *do,*" he said. "Honestly, that's all I *could* do, because as you say I'm not an actor, I don't sing, I don't dance. However, I'm terribly interesting. You see, I only went through tenth grade. But I've read all my life. And I should add that I was light heavyweight wrestling champion in Jackson, Michigan, where I was known as Roughhouse Paar. I remember the championship bout against the Black Panther. I won it. Foolishly, being a liberal, I then gave him a rematch, and it was a big mistake. The black kid beat the hell out of me. I was a sick kid, had tuberculosis, so my father wanted me to be a man and bought me a weight-lifting set. He sent away for a big crate of barbells and apparatus. It came to our home and neither my father or I could lift the box. My mother opened it, I think, then we took the weights out separately. If we put them together we couldn't lift anything."

Jack's eclectic abilities served him well as a host, but what served him best was his ability to be noticed; he somehow managed to turn small incidents into events. He went on:

"People have said that I was a master of public relations as a television performer. I kid you not, I never asked for all of that, and never sought it. But I had a knack of replying quickly to anything that I thought was unfair or untrue or unjust. And so small things grew into controversies, and people thought I wanted that. I didn't. I wanted to be left the hell alone, make some money, raise my family. But there's something about my personality that causes wars. Not just on television, either. I'll give you an example. In the army I was an infantry soldier, not a USO performer. I was a corporal, later became a sergeant, then later became a private. My captain was a Southerner who used to call me in and say, 'Sergeant Paar, I'm bustin' you!' I thought he was a wonderful guy, though.

"But I was a problem to the army because I did entertain the troops and became a very outspoken comedian—there was no such thing in the army then. I was sent to Guadalcanal, traveling forty-three days from Staten Island, scared to death; when I'm nervous I have the knack of saying the most outrageous things and getting away with it. I had some judgment and taste, I knew how far to go, and I had an angelic kind of face. When I made a wild remark, my superiors would say, 'He doesn't *mean* it.' But I meant everything I said. Anyway, I did shows for the troops there and became a bigger success and celebrity in the army than I ever was in civilian life. It's also a question of who *wants* to be big on Guadalcanal, but anyway I guess the army thought my entertainment was good for the men, they knew I wouldn't go too far with it. But one night I did.

"Here's the situation. We were on Mundo, and there were five thousand guys there, sitting on logs; the stage was oil barrels with planks on top. We had a little orchestra, wonderful singers; a hell of a good show for being in the middle of a war. The show was supposed to start at eight. We had a lot of wounded men being brought in from Saipan, and I wanted to make them laugh. The amazing thing was that the men who had lost an arm and a leg, who were carried on stretchers to the show, *could* still laugh; the shock must have happened later.

"I was doing two shows a day for these guys for twenty-eight months, and they always laughed. Anyway, this one night the show couldn't go on. You cannot start any performance until the top officer, whether it is a commander or admiral, is 'piped' in. So now it's eight-twenty and here are these guys with no arms and legs, waiting, and the show couldn't start. Someone whispered to me, 'Don't start the show because the admiral has some girls up in his quonset hut.' They were USO performers, a couple of girl singers. Now the men start clapping. When five thousand men clap in anger the sound gets worse and worse. Finally I said, 'The hell with it, I'm going out there.' I walked out and said into the microphone:

" 'You wouldn't think that the admiral and a couple of broads would keep five thousand guys waiting.'

"That caused a little comment among the brass backstage. I continued, 'I'll tell you what happened.' And then I went too far. 'There are two USO girls here and they were going to do the Dance of Virgins for you tomorrow night, but they went out with the admiral and they broke their contract.'

"Well, I was arrested that moment, right on stage, and locked in a shower room. I begged them to let me at least finish the show, but they didn't. They were going to court-martial me. But my very brave captain stood up for me, so the penalty was being confined to quarters. Well, hell, being confined to quarters on Mundo was hardly a penalty."

When Jack did enter show business formally, and when he took over "The Tonight Show," his ability to cause sensations served him well. He swears it was all by accident, and I believe him, but a talk show host hasn't since made headlines the way Paar used to. For instance, on one of his trips abroad he was involved in an incident at the Berlin Wall that got all the way back to Congress. What actually happened has never been clearly explained, but press reports had Paar order our military stationed there to attack East Germans at the border. I reminded Jack. He flung his hands in the air and said: "That was a disaster from the standpoint of the harm it did to people, based on an absolutely false report in the press. It had no basis in fact, but the New York *Times* covered the story for three days without one true fact." Congressmen, having read the reports in the *Times,* gave speeches criticizing Paar, and at least one suggested he should be banished from America.

"I told Congress to go to hell. I'm the only man I know of who ever said on television, 'The United States Congress can go to hell,' and I meant it because in *this* country you're going to have to prove something when you make charges, you can't just stand up and make speeches about a person. I *didn't* order tanks up to the Berlin Wall, I did *not* order troops to attack the East Germans; the things the press reported were ridiculous. I had my daughter and Peggy Cass standing for an hour and a half at the Berlin Wall; am I likely to start trouble?

"The harmful and vicious part of the incident was that two officers, both highly decorated colonels who had served in Korea and World War II, were practically demoted on the basis of these false reports. Later, the whole incident was investigated by a committee of Congress and they found out that none of the things reported by the press had actually happened. Of course, there were no apologies from the newspapers, just a tiny box in the back of the paper."

Jack's quick wit actually cost him a couple of sponsors for "The Tonight Show." He explained: "You see, it was tough for me because not only did I have to do the show, but in the afternoon had to rehearse all the commercials. You only have so much energy and I'm bored with all the stuff outside the show itself. So I would ad lib once in a while just to break the monotony; we lost some accounts because of it. We had Jockey shorts as a sponsor until I said they fit so tight it was like wearing a slingshot, or being hugged by a midget. We lost them. Manischewitz wine I called 'The Jewish Lavoris,' and we lost that too.

"During my days as an announcer, I was supposed to do a piece about some disease. I would get in front of the camera and read the copy cold, without having seen it. So this announcement started with symptoms, something like, 'Do you wake up in the middle of the night and frequent the bathroom regularly, or too regularly? Do your hands perspire? Do you have a scratching behind the ears? Do you . . .' All I remember was staring at the copy and freezing. The director said, 'Jack, what's wrong?' And I said, 'I have *every* one of those symptoms!'

"I was staring and reading to myself because I couldn't wait to finish and find out what disease I had!"

*

W. CLEMENT STONE—One of America's wealthiest
men:
"Anyone who is truly successful, continuously successful, must
engage in thinking time, planning time and study time with
regularity. Unfortunately, most people won't do that and that's
why they don't succeed."

*

The secret I learned about doing talk shows from Jack Paar
was preparation. Yes, Jack is spontaneous. But when he walked
out on a stage he was prepared. He had a funny little story
ready for his monologue, he had specific questions ready for his
guests. Sometimes he never used his preparation. A guest can
walk out dressed in a manner that surprises you and your
interview goes in an entirely different direction. But you've
something to fall back on. The best hosts know when to let a
show take its own path, and they know when to take control
and give it direction. I appeared on Paar's "The Tonight
Show" many times and was always fascinated to watch his
routine just before show time.

For a few minutes before curtain he stayed alone in a room,
protected by a watchful stage manager. Then the theme would
start, Hugh Downs began his opening announcement and on
cue Jack would stride out of his enclosure without looking left
or right, straight out onto the stage to deliver his monologue.
I asked him the reasons behind the routine, and here is his
explanation:

"I found that reading cue cards during my monologue made
it *sound* like reading, and I don't like that sort of feeling on
stage. So I used to start with the writers about ten in the
morning. The writers would give me jokes and I would contribute some. We'd get it all together and then I'd say, 'Now I
don't want to hear a word from anyone, everyone leave.' And

then I would write it over in longhand, because it went into my brain better that way. That's how I memorized my monologue. Jack Benny used to come on the show and not believe I didn't use cue cards. But I did this eight-, nine-minute monologue night after night. However, you couldn't get in my way when I was ready to go on stage. If someone asked me a question just before the show, I was in trouble.

"I only blanked out once. I had done my routine with the writers, then the longhand and memorization. I went into my private room and then walked out, waiting for Hugh's introduction. Suzy Parker, the model, was standing there, an adorable girl. And I broke the rule.

"I said, 'Darling, how are you?'

" 'I'm getting divorced,' she said.

" 'I'm sorry,' I said. 'How about the children?'

"She shrugged, 'I don't know, who knows?'

"Then Hugh announced, 'Here's Jack!' And I went out on stage and could not think of a thing to say. My entire monologue had disappeared from my head in those few seconds. I just didn't know what to do. So I stared at the audience. Hugh got scared, everybody looked frightened. I said, 'I've been drinking.' Suddenly it fell into a funny patter, and they really thought I was loaded. Hell, I'd rather have them like me as a *drunken* idiot than as just a plain idiot."

*

DICK CAVETT—On his first try as a stand-up comedian: "I found right away there are problems in doing comedy. My major problem my first six months of performing was lack of laughter. It can get on your nerves if it goes on. My first appearance in comedy was at The Bitter End, a club in Greenwich Village. It was my first night and I had twenty minutes of socko material. I went out and I broke the house record for silence. Nobody laughed; it was crucifying, awful and painful.

Nobody laughed and two people burst into tears, and I was one of them."

*

My only fear in life, speaking in a business sense, is waking up in the morning with no desire to go to work, no curiosity about anyone on my show that night. That would signal for me the end of my career in front of the camera. It hasn't happened yet, and I'm hoping it won't. But it was that feeling exactly that caused Jack Paar to step down from "The Tonight Show." He recalls:

"It is generally true in a broad way that I had run out of Oscar Levant, George Kaufman, Dorothy Parker, Alexander King, all the kind of people I loved talking with. Today they don't even know what an Alexander King is; he was one of the most fascinating men you'll ever see on television. And Oscar Levant . . . with him you were seeing a true neurotic genius. George Kaufman and James Thurber were two other greats from my show. I think of the night I said to the audience, 'Here are two unknowns who are going to do something called 'impromptu' which you may or may not understand. Just yell out something and watch what happens.' And out came Mike Nichols and Elaine May, and they were brilliant. Bill Cosby, Carol Burnett, Woody Allen, Jonathan Winters, Joan Rivers, Phyllis Diller, Bob Newhart all started with me, and I was thrilled to be a part of it.

"But I was not always right about talent. They introduced me to this chubby little man, Peter Ustinov. I had never heard of him, no one else in America had either, and I wondered what he could possibly do on my show. Ustinov said, 'I'll think of something.' And Peter Ustinov has been charming this country, and me, for twenty years. But I didn't know it *then*. I'll tell you two instances where I was *very* wrong. I was first to bring the Beatles into this country by film. I saw them in

London and I thought it was a joke; I didn't know they had great music in them. I simply thought they were amusing, and had no idea they were going to revolutionize music. And the other person I could have been wrong about was Marilyn Monroe. I just never understood that child."

Curiously, when I asked Jack which politician he had interviewed who impressed him most, he picked the same man I pick as the most impressive politician ever to guest my show, Bobby Kennedy.

"He had greatness in him," Jack said. "We'll never really know, but I thought there was enormous potential greatness in that man. For all his faults, and he had many, like a very short temper, I think there was a rare quality in Bobby."

Most entertainers and performers dread the thought of slipping from the public eye. It is not a subject I worry about much, because I tend to face each day as a new challenge, splitting my interests between my own show and the shows I produce from the other side of the camera, such as my game show "Wheel of Fortune" and the popular dance show "Dance Fever."

*

BILL RUSSELL—The legendary basketball star of the Boston Celtics, on the night he knew it was time to retire:
"I realized very clearly one night when I should retire. I was player-coach at the time, and we were playing in Baltimore against the Bullets. We get down to the last twenty seconds and the score's tied. We go in the huddle on a time-out and I say, 'We're gonna kill these guys, we're gonna kill 'em, kill 'em!' And then I thought about what I was saying and I started to laugh. So one of the players said, 'Coach, you haven't told

us who's gonna shoot the ball, what kind of shot to take, how much time we're gonna use on the clock, you haven't told us anything, you're standing here laughing. What are you laughing about?' And I said, 'I feel silly. I'm standing here, I'm thirty-five years old, standing here semi-nude in front of ten thousand people, talking about killing somebody in a god-damned basketball game. And I feel silly as hell!' "

*

Jack Paar seems perfectly contented with his life away from the spotlight. He's been happily married for thirty-six years, and Jack and Miriam's daughter Randy is "now a great young citizen. Married, a graduate of Harvard, a lawyer and she has been mugged four times, which makes her a citizen."

"My own day," Jack explained, "is very simple. Between nine and eleven I take a ride in the car with the dog and listen to the radio. At eleven Miriam and I have a bottle of champagne, then lunch. After that I paint. Before I know it, it's four o'clock, time for a little tennis, some champagne, then dinner. I watch the news, take a look to see who's on *your* show, then read until eleven. I don't look back on the television days with great nostalgia. It was tough going. But I am very grateful for it. I'd never knock the business because there is no reason for me to. But it is not a thing I need to go on living." He flashed the patented Paar grin. "I have nothing booked now but dying. That's going to be the next great event in my life. Look, someone once wrote, 'Does Jack Paar think he can walk on water?' I thought about it once, went down to the Hudson River and figured if I *could* do it, I would only end up in Newark. Why get the bottoms of my socks wet for Newark?"

During the closing ceremonies of our tennis tournament in Monaco, I presented Prince Rainier and the late Princess

Grace with a small gift. It was a miniature television set, not much larger than a pack of cigarettes. They were thrilled with the little gadget. Then we boarded our plane and returned to America. A few weeks after our return I received a note from Jack Paar with a clipping from an electronics catalogue attached to it. All he said in the note was, 'Thought you might like to see this.' The catalogue displayed the miniature television I'd given the Royal Family. I couldn't figure out what Jack had in mind, until I read the catalogue copy. It contained all the specifications and marvelous claims but at the bottom in type so small I needed a magnifying glass to read it were the words: "Important Note: This unit will not operate in Brazil, Poland or Monaco."

I sent Jack a letter in return. My only words were: "Your note is precisely why you should still be on television."

BURT REYNOLDS
A Revealing Personality

As I was walking offstage one night, shortly after I'd moved my show from New York to Hollywood in 1970, a talent manager approached me looking distraught. He told me one of his clients was about to leave him, but that if he could get the young actor a booking on my show he might be able to save the relationship. The manager was almost in tears, and since I knew he was a good man, I said, fine, we'd use the young actor if he had a decent personality. Great personality, the manager said; he's not famous but he's very funny about himself. Fine then, I told him, we'd do the favor. And that's how I first met Burt Reynolds.

Right from the start he was a smash. The audience wasn't quite sure who he was, but Burt was so funny talking about his life, and particularly his failures in show business, that he became one of our most popular guests. He appeared with us twenty times; then, once the Cosmopolitan magazine centerfold hit, followed by the movie "Deliverance," Burt was launched as an international cinema superstar.

"I gambled with that Cosmopolitan thing," Burt remembers, "I really gambled. The gamble was would I be considered a serious actor after that. When I died, would they write on my tombstone, 'His contribution to the world was he did the first male nude centerfold?' And I never ever would have done it had I not had 'Deliverance' finished and in the can, which is a fact most people don't realize. 'Deliverance' was 'B.C.', *before* Cosmopolitan. I felt that I had the sense of humor to handle it, to handle all the barbs I was going to get afterwards. I certainly didn't think it was a lascivious piece of pornography. I just thought it was a funny takeoff on Playboy. My parents didn't think it was dirty, though a lot of other people did. A lot of people said, 'Well, if it wasn't for that, he wouldn't be in the position that he is in pictures.' But that's such a naive, stupid statement. I mean, obviously, if one could take one's clothes off, as one does quite often, get one's picture taken and put in the magazine and they could become a movie star by doing it, we'd have people dropping their drawers all over the world, wouldn't we? That's just not the way it happens. I remember once being in a restaurant and a guy who was playing a violin walked over and said, 'Boy, that Cosmopolitan thing really did it for you; I mean, you were nothing before that.' I said, 'Yeah, that's true. Why don't you take your clothes off and pose in the magazine and then you can play Carnegie Hall!' "

Burt is one of the handful of actors who truly understand talkshows. He isn't afraid to reveal himself, to let people get a look at his personality. Many actors are afraid to talk about themselves; they believe that people won't take them seriously as actors unless they talk only *about* acting. But I think Burt has won such a wide audience for his films not only because he can act, which he can do very well, but also because television viewers respond to his personality, his humor and warmth. They *like* him, and will pay to see him at work. It was always interesting to watch the audience during Burt's first appearances on my show; they weren't too familiar with his work, but he told them stories they could empathize with, and clearly people felt he was a guy you could know.

He used to talk about growing up, and he always got laughs. "I grew up in a happy family. I don't think anybody really knows they are poor, until somebody says, 'Hey, aren't *you* poor?' If you've got a great relationship with your family and if you've got religion, which we did, and if you have enough to eat, then you're not poor. I used to be embarrassed when I went to grammar school; most of the guys I liked were all barefooted, some of them because they simply couldn't afford shoes. So I used to go to school with my shoes on and then take them off and hide them under a bush so I'd be cool. Then after school on my home I would put them back on. My dad used to say, 'Man, you really take care of them shoes.' One pair lasted three years.

"My favorite song in high school, and also the song of my favorite girl, Mary Ellis, was 'My Secret Love.' Unfortunately, at the time I was dating another girl from college, we were secretly going out, and one night 'My Secret Love' came on and she said, 'I love that song, it reminds me of you,' and that became *our* song, too.

"And then I was sneaking down to Lake Worth once in a while, dating a cheerleader, and she fell in love with 'My Secret Love.' Unfortunately, one night the four girls got together at one of the hangouts and 'My Secret Love' came on and at the same time they all said, 'That's Buddy's and my song.' Needless to say, I never saw those girls again, except for Mary Ellis."

At times, Burt gives the impression on television of being a swaggering, wise-cracking man's man; that's the part of his personality that gets the laughs. But I've had the opportunity to see a different side of him, a more interesting one. After his popularity exploded in the early seventies, my company produced a television special featuring Burt called "Take Me Home Again," and for the show we did exactly that, we went down to Florida with Burt to visit the areas where he grew up and spent his youth. Once he was on his home turf, one saw the inner Burt Reynolds, a deeply emotional, sensitive man who considers his roots the foundation of his life.

*

ALAN ALDA:
"I think that work in your personal life is just as important as work in your professional life. I don't think you can have intimate relationships with the people you think you love unless you work very hard on them. I think a lot of us think that stuff takes care of itself, or can come later. People will say, 'I'm going to become successful. Here's my opportunity. I'm going to seize this opportunity and then, *later*, I'll come back to the family.' And ten years later the family is either very changed, or they're not there."

*

"The most important thing in the world to me," Burt told us, "now and always has been, are the friends that I have, the ones that I grew up with—they are terribly important to me. That's why I just keep coming back home. I don't want to have a relationship with people that's based upon whether my rating on my latest television show went up or down, or whether the newest movie is in the top ten. It's great to have a relationship with somebody just because you love 'em and they love you, and they knew you before it all happened, and if it all just stopped tomorrow they would still care about you. I mean, they're happy that I'm doing well, but they're doing great in their professions too. What the hell difference does it make if my profession is the movies and theirs is schoolteaching or selling, or being a baker or whatever. I'm just as proud of them as they are of me. I know they may not believe this, but I am.

*

KEMMONS WILSON—Founder of Holiday Inns:
"Success is not money. Success is being happy with what you're

doing. I think you're extremely successful if you're happy doing what you want to do. Everybody thinks that when you get successful, and the money that comes with it, you have the 'end answer.' It isn't. Money is the most unimportant thing in the world. You've got to live the way you want to live. For some people that's $25,000 a year, for some it's $50,000 a year. But anything above that is just a way of keeping score."

*

"I guess the most embarrassing thing that ever happened to me in front of the guys was when I was a junior in high school, playing football against Jacksonville. It was a very important game, and we had the ball at the opening. The first play was a pass to me, and I streaked down field wide open; we should have had a touchdown, but as I was stepping across the goal-line, reading my name in the paper the next day, I was tipped from behind and blew the play. We lost the game by six points. At the end of the year our coach said, 'We could have had a good record except for a young man there who is slow, little and has no guts.' And then he pointed at me."

Burt makes jokes now about dropping the big touchdown pass in high school, especially since the next year he was one of the stars of his championship team. But incidents like the one he described stay with a person. Interestingly, there is another top box-office star who once described a similar incident to me. He had played on his school's varsity basketball team during his junior year; he wasn't one of the starters, but he practiced hard, and got into a game now and then. At the awards ceremony at the end of the season, the team was introduced to the student body and parents and given their block sweaters. But when this young man was introduced, he was given not a block sweater but a "certificate of achievement," because, despite the fact that he'd worked and sweated out the season with the rest of the guys, he hadn't played long enough in league games to earn the block. Years later he said his drive to achieve, to be recognized and applauded on the screen by people the world over, derived from that one humiliating moment. He avoided the team party, went home after the ceremony, locked himself in his room and cried, vowing he would never feel "left out" in front of the public again.

When Burt Reynolds first came to Hollywood he suffered one of those awful moments that seem to stay with a person forever.

"When I went to Hollywood everybody wanted me to meet Marlon Brando—when you're a young actor you hear so many Brando stories. There was a coffee house on Sunset Strip called Cyrano's, and at the time it was the 'in' place. Everybody went there to see or be seen. I had a date with a lovely girl named Sandy Stockwell, and we wandered into Cyrano's. By then I'd done a few things as an actor, and had kind of a rebellious reputation. As we walked in, a director I knew ran over and grabbed me and said, 'He's here!'

"I said, 'Who is?'

"And he said, 'Come on.'

"I thought it must be Albert Schweitzer; I mean, who could it be that this guy was so excited about, pulling me by the shirt. Everybody in the restaurant was watching this director dragging a guy around the room. We stopped in front of a table where three guys were sitting, one of whom, I realized, was Marlon Brando. Everybody at the table was looking at me, except for Marlon; he was looking away at an angle. The director said, 'Marlon, isn't this fantastic!' And, like a dummy, I'm just kind of smiling, thinking I'd been brought over to be introduced. I didn't realize this guy thought I was a lookalike and I was being brought over to be shown. Marlon probably has young actors thrust upon him all the time, and he must have thought, Here's some other dummy who thinks he looks like me, but he never looked up, quietly grunted.

"I was standing there with my hand extended over the table, and there was this deathly silence and suddenly I had the urge to kill. To reach across the table and kill. And I ran out of the restaurant, went right past poor Sandy, jumped in the car and drove around the hills saying, 'I'll kill that son of a bitch. I mean, who does he think I *am*? Does he think I got to be an actor because I look like *him*'? When I attended the Actors Studio there were seventy-five Marlon Brandos and eight James Deans, and I just left. I wanted to be me. And I was now steamed. 'Who the hell does he think I am, being rude to me like that. I extended my hand . . .' So I drove to Brando's house and waited for him, figuring that when he drove up I'd tell him off. But, unfortunately, he never came home and I never saw him again."

*

SIDNEY POITIER—On becoming an actor:
"I never asked anyone's opinion whether I should be an actor or not, just because at that time, with the historical circumstances being what they were, I would have been told not to do it. It was determination on my part; not to be just an actor, but to be the best. I have not succeeded, but at least I set my star so high that I would constantly be in motion toward it."

*

Burt has hit just about every goal he's ever aimed at in life, and done so with style and humor. Two goals still elude him. One is to win an Oscar, something he doesn't talk about much —every actor craves the appreciation of his peers. The second goal is to have kids.

"The only thing I'm really lacking in my life," he said, "is that I desperately want to have kids. It isn't an ego thing, I don't want a 'Burt, Jr.' Quite honestly, I'd like to adopt some kids, but my particular image is unbearably bad for adopting kids. First of all, actors are the worst risk, single actors especially. I have in my mind that when I have a baby I'm going to have to get married. But marriage. . . often it's people together who really hate each other or are bored. If they're living together, without the license hanging on the wall, they can split any time they want, so they're really together because they *want* to be, and that's a terrific arrangement. That's why I'm screwed up. I'm either going to have to adopt a kid or get married, one of the two. I just want to have a kid who understands the place I come from, calls it home and wants to go back there with me."

I'm sure, knowing Burt, that his dream will come true, and Burt will be very happy, just as long as no one tells him his kid looks like Marlon Brando.

MOVIES AND THEIR MAKERS

*

LIV ULLMANN—Describing the work of her former husband, filmmaker Ingmar Bergman:
"He's a very personal artist, and I think like all great artists he writes his scripts and makes his movies out of his own anxiety. Maybe his movies are not entirely for entertainment. But if you are interested to see what happens inside a human being, things which you might recognize inside yourself, then I think an Ingmar Bergman film would be a new experience. And you could go to the movies knowing that they can be entertainment, but something else too; something you feel and learn from."

*

ALFRED HITCHCOCK
The Genius of Suspense

OF ALL THE great film directors I have interviewed, only one possessed a personality as famous as his films. Show any film fan a pencil outline of his features, and the name Alfred Hitchcock comes immediately to mind. He looked as though he'd never had a day's exercise in his life, and probably he hadn't; the thought of putting on sweat clothes and jogging shoes and trotting about the neighborhood was as distasteful to him as the notion of "eating" as opposed to "dining." Hitch was a man of the mind.

When his mind was engaged, he was awesome to observe. To the public he seemed aloof, unemotional, but that was his pose. I watched him at work one day on the set of "I Confess," in which he was directing Montgomery Clift and Karl Malden. On a movie set the director is king. He is responsible for motivating and maintaining the vision of the film, juggling the hundreds of elements involved in the creation of any movie, integrating them into a final work that is all of a piece, rather than the patchwork fabric it is. This requires careful planning prior to shooting and intense concentration during the process, two qualities for which Hitchcock was famous. Hitchcock planned his movies meticulously. He believed that to create suspense on film each element of the story must be consistent and correct, the details must work. As he told me, if he was going to use a crop duster in a scene, as he did in "North by Northwest," it must *dust*, not simply *look* like it might. On the set of "I Confess" I saw both his planning and concentration at work. A scene was in preparation, and Hitchcock studied the set carefully, considering his camera angles, looking at what would be included in the shot. If there was a paperweight on the desk, close to where an actor was to sit, then there must be a purpose and use for it. He was very quiet. He spoke to the actors almost in a whisper. As the filming began, he leaned forward in his chair, his eyes mirroring the emotion of the scene. It was as if he were living each line of dialogue as the actors spoke it; the rhythm of his breathing increased as the scene progressed. There could have been a boxing match going on next to him and I don't think he would have noticed, so complete was his concentration. His instructions to crew and actors were brief, often one word, but everyone understood him, obviously because a great deal of thought had gone into the one word he chose to use.

I was not introduced to him on the set that day. We met twenty years later—when he came to my show. As he shook my hand I saw the same thought process occurring in his eyes as I had witnessed on the film set; clearly he was considering some aspect of me. I waited for him to reveal what it was.

"I was rather disturbed," he said, "when I heard you were referred to as 'Merv.' " He let me ponder that a moment, then continued: " 'Mr. Mervyn Griffin' . . . it seems more *dig*nified. When I sees signs like 'Norm's Drive-In' or 'Erv's Garage,' well, the dignity of the thing concerns me, because we might get to Washington, D.C., and we'll find things like 'Dick's Government.' When I first noticed the name of a leading lady who had a Christian name with no initial letter, Lizabeth Scott, I began to wonder what could *other* names be like if we took the first letter away. Of course, the first person I thought of was 'Reer' Garson, then there was 'Ary' Grant, 'Lark' Gable,

'Rank' Sinatra, 'Ickey' Rooney. The dignified use of your name is essential, Mr. Mervyn Griffin; not *'Merv.'* "

I recalled my day on the set of "I Confess," and remarked on his economy of words with the actors. "I get on very well with actors. I think it is a very lowly profession, however. But they can't help that. I've called them cattle for years. I was giving a speech once, and I said the legend that gets around that I consider all actors cattle is absolutely untrue; I'd never stoop so low as to say a mean thing like that. What I probably said was all actors should be *treated* like cattle. You see, they're children. They are playing house. They're pretending. They put stuff on their faces and pretend to be someone else. That's what acting *is.*"

Hitchcock's comments about actors were meant primarily in jest—the respect he had for actors like Montgomery Clift was obvious—but I must say there is some truth in his words. When I was a film actor, briefly, in 1952, what I remember best about the experience is feeling *silly.* Pretending to be someone else just never made sense to me, and that's at least one of the reasons there are no Oscars on my mantel. Interestingly, John Derek told me he had the same feeling about acting. These days, Derek is best known for having been married to Ursula Andress, Linda Evans and now Bo. But he was certainly one of the screen's most dashing leading men.

*

JOHN DEREK—On directing his wife, Bo Derek, in "Tarzan":
"I thought Bo would be terrible and phony and I'd end up sending her back to California with her surfboard. But she surprised me with an incredible naturalness that comes right through the lens. It's the hardest kind of acting to do, and I found that she did it remarkably well."

*

"I just wasn't comfortable with it," he told me one afternoon at his ranch, "putting on silly costumes, going into the
makeup room and having people fuss with your face and hair.
To tell you the truth, it didn't seem a masculine thing to do.
Playacting. I got to feeling it was just something women are
more comfortable with, so I got out of it and put myself on the
other end of the camera."

Despite Hitchcock's feelings about the acting profession,
now and then he put himself in front of the camera and his
cameo appearances became a trademark. Some fans went to
Hitchcock pictures just so they could see how he was going to
reveal himself.

"That started about the third picture," he recalled. "We ran
out of actors, so I had to suffer the indignity of being an actor.
Perhaps my most unusual appearance was in 'Lifeboat.' It was
in the middle of the ocean. William Bendix was reading the
newspaper in the boat, and there was an ad on the back of the
paper. It was an ad for some stuff called 'Reducer,' and it
showed me before and after. I regret to say that I have now
reverted to before. I took off one hundred pounds for that
'after' shot. I suppose in my lifetime I must have taken off at
least five hundred pounds. Where it *is*, I don't know."

As Orson Welles pointed out to me, the best films require
the viewer to bring his imagination actively into play. And that
is why Hitchcock's films weather the test of time. The majority
of today's thrillers and suspense films appeal to voyeurs rather
than viewers; they use excessive graphic violence in place of
plot. Filmmakers sense their audiences are jaded and in need
of shock treatments to elict any response. But Hitchcock forces
us to use our wits to anticipate the twists of his plots. Mystery
did not matter to him; suspense did.

"It's very simple. Mystery is what it means: you mystify the audience. You have a group of characters, one of them is the murderer. Reading a book you are tempted to turn to the last page and have a look. There's no emotion to that. There's only emotion with suspense, anxiety. You, the audience, must go through emotions, but you can't go through emotions without the information. It's as simple as that. Mysteries are nothing, they are like crossword puzzles. It's much more important to *know* who the murderer is, and then want to call out to the girl in the scene, 'Don't go with him, whatever you do.'

"I've always kept in mind the fusing term of a bomb. You and I could be talking for five minutes, suddenly the bomb goes off and we're blown to smithereens. Ten seconds of shock for the audience. But if you tell the audience five minutes *ahead* that there is a bomb under the desk, now the state of mind of the audience is *totally* different. Audiences, if I may so say without offending anyone, are most peculiar people. Answer this: Supposing a man is robbing a woman's jewelry in an upstairs bedroom. He's got the drawer open. Suddenly the camera goes downstairs and shows the woman coming into her house, closing the door quietly behind her in the hallway below. What will the audience say to the criminal? 'Hurry up, get out, you're going to get caught!' They're all criminals, the whole lot. The eleventh commandment is: 'Thou shalt not be found out.' "

Hitchcock mastered the ability to let us know *something* was going to happen, and let the suspense build as we waited to find out *how* it would happen. The greatest example was "North by Northwest."

"The point is," he said, "you want to avoid the cliché. That comes in the writing. In every gangster film, for example, you have the scene where the man is put on the spot. Now, what's the convention? The man stands under a street lamp at night. The cobbles are washed with recent rain. A black cat slithers along. Somebody opens the curtains and peers out from his apartment. A limousine with a gunman goes by. It's a cliché. I would do it in bright sunshine, no trees, no house, nothing. You then have the audience wondering, Where is it coming from? And sure enough, this crop duster eventually comes down and shoots at him. He runs into the cornfield, so it dusts him out. It dusts him into the road and then there is a smashup with a train.

"Now, that was done to avoid the cliché. Then I saw a picture called 'From Russia with Love,' and you have Sean Connery chased by a helicopter. Then you see a film called 'That Man from Rio,' and the hero is chased by a motorboat. And another film comes along called 'Z,' where an automobile chases a man on the sidewalk. So what I did to avoid the cliché *becomes* the cliché."

Because he was a master of imagination, Hitchcock could manipulate our emotions with the deftness of a symphony conductor. The fear and horror you feel watching the famous shower scene in "Psycho" is a cinematic accomplishment, as opposed to the shock of a contemporary film in which the actors have fake limbs severed by chain saws.

"It took one week to shoot that scene," Hitchcock recalled, "which lasted only forty-five seconds in the movie. The prop department made me the loveliest torso of rubber. They tubed it inside with blood, and wherever you stabbed the knife, blood would gush out. I never used that, it's too obvious and too vulgar. Actually, the whole film was made in black and white in the interests of good taste. Had I made it in color, with all that blood flowing down . . . well, it wasn't necessary. To achieve good taste you don't have to do the violence with all the blood. It's the ingenuity of the creator to get all the menace he can into it. But not necessarily doing it on the nose. It's what one might term the minimum of effort and the maximum of effect. I had a letter from a man who wrote, 'My daughter, after seeing the French film "Diabolique," would never use the bathtub. Now, having seen "Psycho," she won't take a shower, and she's getting very unpleasant to be around. What shall I do?' I wrote back, 'Dear Sir, send her to the dry cleaners.' "

Hitchcock expressed to me the same attitude about using sex in his films as he did about the use of violence. "I don't believe in the sexy blonde, it's too obvious for me, with their sex hanging in front of them like jewelry. It must emerge in story fashion. You don't look at every woman and judge, 'She's sexy, she's not.' You must find it out."

*

SOPHIA LOREN—On beauty:
"Beauty is not a static condition. I think beauty emanates from a person. You can see beautiful eyes, but if they don't say anything, if they don't radiate something from your soul and your being, then they don't mean anything. There is no beauty if there is no personality."

On aging:
"I never think about age. Never. I think you have to get along with the years and look the best you can, and be free to be the age that you are. Otherwise, you go out of your mind. The years go by; there's nothing you can do about it."

*

That is why I find the sexiest movies of all time to be classics like "Laura," with Gene Tierney, and "Casablanca." The sexual undertones are woven into the story, created by careful plotting and brilliant dialogue. It is the style of filmmaking most appreciated, I think, by those of us who grew up in the radio era, where our minds worked overtime to imagine the scenes we heard being played out. The sexiest scene in a movie can be a couple dining in a romantic restaurant, with the director capturing their subtle, inviting gestures and their escalating interest in each other, all built by dialogue. It hardly seems necessary, then, for the camera to follow the couple home and watch them reenact the *Kama Sutra.*

I'll give you an example. I did a cameo appearance in the film "Rich and Famous," which starred Jacqueline Bisset and Candice Bergen. When I watched the film, there was a scene where Bisset is on an airplane returning from Los Angeles to New York, and she is engaged in conversation by her handsome seatmate. Because of the emotional state she is in, he gradually seduces her, and ends up having sex with her, clearly with some discomfort, in the plane's bathroom. The scene made its point clearly when he stepped into the bathroom with Miss Bisset and closed the door; and one was hard pressed to understand why the director, one of the giants of cinema, George Cukor, felt it necessary for the audience to see the pair trying to have sex. It concerns me that today's audiences find such overstatement palatable.

The careful creation of Hitchcock's plots emerged from his lifelong fascination with crime. "The English have always paid much more interest to the literature of crime than any other country," he told me. "Go back to Conan Doyle and Sherlock Holmes. The English have always had very bizarre crimes, extremely bizarre crimes. This man Cristie stashed up eight dead bodies all over the house. That's what I would call a touch of domesticity. And the Moors case, now *that* was a dreadful one. That was a young couple who murdered a lot of children, and played back their cries on tape recordings. I am apprised of the great crimes, completely. I use them. For 'Rear Window' I took an item from Dr. Crippen. He was a murderer discovered in a very simple way. He said his wife had gone abroad, but they noticed his secretary was wearing the wife's jewelry. That's all it was. Simple.

"I don't think one has favorite crimes; one has famous, dramatic *moments* of crime. For example, in 'Rear Window,' do you recall the man who kept going away with the suitcase? In there were pieces of the body of the victim. That came from a real case. He had a problem with the head. If you noticed in 'Rear Window,' the head is buried in the garden. That was taken from a real case. The detective on the case— I used him later as a technical advisor—told me that the criminal tried to burn the head of the woman he'd murdered in the fireplace. And the heat of the fire, as the head burned, caused the eyes to open. Can you imagine that? He ran out screaming."

When Hitchcock came to appear on my show, the audience looked at him with awe, as though he were not a real person. That response amused him. Often when I'm interviewing someone with a highly defined public personality, they let down their act during commercial breaks. Truman Capote, for example, is much more dramatic and animated when the red light on top of the camera goes on than he is during a break. But Hitchcock remained consistent. During the commercials he would continue to chat with me about what we'd been discussing on the air, and his use of language and his dry wit never varied. I asked him during a commercial if he enjoyed his personal fame, and he told me a story that I coaxed him to repeat when we returned to the air.

"Autograph hounds are rotten," he said, glaring at the audience with his deadpan delivery. "The most peculiar autograph I was ever requested to give came when I was standing in the main square in Copenhagen. I wasn't shooting a film, I was just looking around, planning some shooting for the future. Suddenly there was an ambulance at the far corner of the square,

siren going, and it pulled up in the middle of the square. A man
jumped out, rushed to me with a pencil and paper and said,
'Autograph, please.' So I gave it to him. He got back into the
ambulance, slammed the door, started the siren again and off
he went. I've never known to this day who the autograph was
for, the patient or the driver."

The last question I ever asked Alfred Hitchcock was, I believe, appropriate for the king of crime and suspense: "Is there
such a thing as the perfect crime?"

"Yes," he said, looking away from me toward the audience,
"and it's being committed this very moment. It's being committed everywhere. And you know why it is the perfect crime?"
He paused, then turned back to face me. "It's never found
out."

ORSON WELLES (II)
Memories of a "Boy Wonder"

SET BACK FROM the street on Melrose Avenue in Los Angeles is a converted house with a tented-over patio out front called Ma Maison. At lunch time, Monday through Friday, it becomes an unofficial film studio commissary, attracting a collection of the industry's most powerful executives, directors, producers, writers and actors, all watched over by the roving eye of the proprietor, Patrick Terrail. Most of the customers prefer to eat in the patio area, since there are only five tables inside, and the best of those five tables is occupied daily by one of Ma Maison's most loyal and famous customers, Orson Welles. Orson likes the bistro atmosphere of the restaurant; it reminds him of France, and he enjoys the *nouvelle cuisine* Ma Maison is famous for. But what I think he enjoys most is the good conversation that goes with good food. It is fitting that the film industry's "house" restaurant should include Orson Welles as one of its feature attractions.

About once a month I'll meet him there for lunch, making an exception to my usual rule of not socializing with the guests who appear on my show. I'm not good at faking interest in a conversation, and if I've had dinner with someone the night before I'm not interested in repeating our conversation on television the next day. But Orson is so damned interesting, I'd never forgive myself if I didn't accept his gracious invitations for food and talk. He eats sparingly at lunch, a light white fish with vegetables, washed down with Perrier water or a glass of wine. Then out comes one of his mammoth Macunudo cigars, and the conversation begins in earnest. At lunch he is the same larger than life character you see on television; Orson is not one to chitchat about the difficulty of finding a good laundry. He likes to address himself to the same interesting topics he pursues on my show.

We were discussing films and filmmaking at lunch one day and he made a statement I found fascinating. I had asked him about working in black and white as opposed to color, and he said, "You know, Merv, no great performance by an actor has ever been given on film in color." Like Alfred Hitchcock, Orson will make a dramatic statement such as that, and then pause, allowing you to reflect about what you *don't* know, before providing the answer.

"I think up to now," he continued, puffing on his cigar, "the *great* performances, which are very few ('great' should be used sparingly, except when we are being complimentary to each other in public; the truth of it is, there are few 'great' *anythings*), the few that are masterpieces have been in black and white for the reason that black and white is more effective for an actor. There's something that color takes away from a performance, and now they are desperately trying to take the color *out* of color; notice how movies today are turning brown and gray and even so dark you don't know who's talking some of the time. All of that is trying to get back to the strength of black and white.

"The real magic of the world, the real magic of theater and movies, is removing some literal thing (like color) and forcing the audience to contribute something poetic. The silent movies, by removing both color and sound, had a kind of magic we'll never catch again. We should never have given them up.

We should have had both silent movies and talking movies, just as we have watercolors and oil paintings. But we gave up silent movies thinking they were a backward step. The last silent movies, like 'The Crowd,' by King Vidor, are pictures that will stand up fifty years from now. Then along came sound. I went to the opening of the first talking picture, and my father, who had been going to silent movies since they were invented—he'd always gone to the movies in the afternoon to fall asleep—got one load of this gala occasion, got up, walked up the aisle and never went to a movie again."

Orson Welles's "Citizen Kane" is certainly the greatest debut of a filmmaker in the history of American cinema. In this film Welles, who was only twenty-six, took on the country's most powerful media magnate, William Randolph Hearst, by delivering a stunning film of enduring popularity. He was the dashing boy wonder I had read about in the papers; he was also a director, actor and writer. From the outside it looked like a spectacular crest of success, but from the inside, Orson explained to me, the view was of a mottled landscape.

"Boy wonder," he said, "was a very common word in those days. I was the boy wonder because then you couldn't find a director who was under sixty years old; today, you can't find one who is *over* twenty-two. But at the time for a kid of twenty-six to be writing, directing, producing and starring in a picture of which he had the final cut and absolute word . . . well, that irritated a lot of people who would have liked a contract like that themselves. So 'boy wonder' was often used, at least in my case, in derision rather than as compliment."

And the fame accorded him with the completion of "Citizen Kane" turned to infamy when Hearst learned the picture was reputedly about him. "All the city editors in America came down on me," Orson remembers. "To what extent Hearst directed it, I don't know. I don't know how much malice he had. But he came down on me. I was vilified in the entertainment press, especially by Louella Parsons, who *had* been so nice to me. She came from a town where I had spent part of my youth and where Ronald Reagan did too, Dixon, Illinois. As a sort of midwesterner, Louella looked kindly on me. She came down to the set of 'Kane' and wrote a glowing piece about what was going on. Then Hedda Hopper broke the news that my movie was supposed to be about Hearst, and everything changed. I was lecturing in Buffalo and was told a policeman was waiting backstage to see me. I turned white—I guess I have a guilty conscience. I went to see him and he told me not to go back to my hotel room. I asked why, and he explained 'they' had an underage girl there in the closet, waiting to jump out and be photographed with me. That would have meant jail for me."

After the "Kane" commotion Orson spent many years in Spain and Italy as an expatriate artist, trying to make films without the technical and financial resources of Hollywood. It is a shame he will not leave a legacy of a dozen films, rather than the few he has made. The cinema needs the big-stakes gamblers like Welles, the type who doesn't play it safe with subject matter or technique. But in these conservative times, when movie studios talk more about cash flow than films, mavericks like Welles are not in favor. I asked him once if he felt cut off from the mainstream of moviemaking.

"The answer is that most people, I suppose, think of me as an actor, while I think of myself as a director. I began directing fifty years ago. I had my own theater in New York. I directed in radio and then in films. But I make the kind of films people do not want to finance. The first films I made were under an extraordinarily lucky contract, which was written because of my radio success and because the head of the studio who signed it didn't know anything about making movies; he only knew about distribution. I had the freedom that was never given again. In order to keep that freedom I have, through the years, done in films what I used to do in the theater, which is to put the money I earned from acting into the movies I direct."

Of course, this is contrary to one of the basic rules of show business, perhaps all business, which is do not risk your own money. Today a filmmaker like George Lucas, who has made staggeringly large profits on "Star Wars" and "The Empire Strikes Back," is in a position to finance his own films, but he is an exception. Orson has always poured his own profits into his projects.

"I lived for over twenty years in Europe because it used to be that an American did not pay income tax unless he lived in his own country. But John Kennedy, responding to the bad publicity of Elizabeth Taylor's million-dollar salary for 'Cleopatra,' changed the law and we had to start paying taxes on top of the taxes we were paying abroad. That, plus the fact that my perfectly legitimate producing company was not believed by the IRS, put a stop to my ability to make enough money to finance my own films. This is *not* an age of mom and pop stores, is it? It's an age of supermarkets and chain stores, and that has affected movies too. Conglomerates make movies, and the whole scene is against the entrepreneur."

Yes and no. The entrepreneur is, indeed, an endangered species, but has not completely vanished. I'll talk about Francis Coppola shortly, one of the new breed of film maverick-entrepreneurs.

What Orson sees, however, goes beyond the lack of individual entrepreneurs in the film industry. He questions the state of the art itself. "We've come to a point in filmmaking where it is impossible to progress any further. All we can do is make another good film, or another *great* film. But we're not going to move the art forward until the technology changes again, when we have the big movie at home, or holographs or any of the things that are seconds away from us. The world today is full of brilliant young directors, people whom I admire beyond words [Coppola and Steven Spielberg are two he admires].

"When I say there's a dead end, I don't mean that the young people aren't up to making the films that were made earlier. I mean the medium has exhausted itself in a way. All we can do is repeat ourselves. This may be sour grapes, justifying my own difficulties in making movies; I see that as a possibility. But if it is sour grapes, it still counts for me, and it still makes sense. I have to say that I have doubted, since the first movie I made, that I could do anything except show that I can still do it. Now, who wants to show that you can still do it? Maybe you do when you are forty and you begin worrying about middle age, but when you start worrying about old age, showing you can still do it is a concern that should be behind you."

What is frustrating for any creative person are the complications involved in producing their art, and filmmaking is one of the most complicated art forms in existence. My own production company, which for twenty years has been creating and producing television shows and is now dipping its feet into the feature film realm, gives me some insight into this problem. I will sit at a lunch with the president of my company and the head of a large television studio, and we will agree on a project we all want to make into a TV show. We will walk away with the glow of a creative meeting, and head with enthusiasm toward the first day of shooting. In the meantime, the deal is turned over to lawyers and accountants for analysis and structuring. And sometimes the wait is endless. With films, millions of dollars and careers are at stake, and nothing moves forward quickly.

"I belong to a profession," Orson pointed out to me, "in which ninety-five percent of one's time and energy goes into getting 'the deal' together in order to do it. The most successful director spends more time getting it together than he does directing. The mechanics of moviemaking are too cumbersome. It takes too long to make them; they're too expensive. As you know, I began as a musician, and I gave it up when my mother died, then I studied to be a painter. I regret now I was unable to go on with my music, and I wonder if I shouldn't have been a painter, because painters lead such happy lives. There have been unhappy painters, but more painters are happy than in any other profession. Chagall, the last great one alive, and Miro, they are very happy men. Picasso was a very happy man. As a painter, you get up in the morning, clean your brushes and go to work all by yourself; and it doesn't cost that much to buy your box of paints. *My* box of paints as a filmmaker costs millions of dollars."

*

SALVADOR DALI—The great painter, on himself: "Compare the painting of Dali with a masterpiece of the Renaissance period, with Velazquez or Raphael, and at that moment Dali is absolutely nothing. Believe that today, though, the best painter is Dali. Dali is only good because the other painters are so bad."

*

"Getting the deal together" has taken on new meaning in the Hollywood of the eighties. Because of the soaring costs of filmmaking, good ideas and capable filmmakers are not enough to get projects off and flying. Bankers want to see marketing reports and demographic studies supporting the appeal of an idea or a star *before* the millions are lent out. In fact, so much nuts-and-bolts information is necessary to attract film money, it's a wonder more of the films that do get made aren't hits. In the thirties, forties and fifties, films were made on the judgment of a studio chief, who also retained the right of editing the final product. That's the way Orson liked to make deals. And he recalled for me one of his most famous.

"I decided to do a musical comedy called *Around the World in Eighty Days* on stage. I wanted to use Cole Porter for the music. Everybody said Cole Porter was washed up, written out, because he hadn't had any successes for a while. But nobody with that genius is ever finished. Cole Porter worked hard on it and we had a good book and a funny show. We had everything except one single song anybody could remember for a minute. The *next* show Cole wrote was *Kiss Me Kate*, which will give you an idea of how *unwritten* out he was. But we were unlucky with the music. We *were* lucky in that we were able to open the show at all, and then only because Mike Todd was our producer.

"We got ten days into rehearsal and suddenly Mike announced he was going bankrupt. I found myself playing the role of Dick Powell in one of those old musicals where there's no money and he says to a cast, 'Kids, we'll put on a show anyway!' I saw all these poor actors and singers and dancers—we had a huge cast—who would be out of work, so I put all my money in it, along with some of Sir Alexander Korda's. We made it to Boston for opening night. We had this enormous cast, a show with twenty-three scenes, and our costumes were being held at the railway station until we could put up fifty thousand dollars for their release. I went back to the theater and looked at the house manager, but he gave me the empty pockets sign. So I was standing in the box office, thinking, 'Who can send me fifty thousand dollars within an hour? Who has the courage and the power to?' And I thought of a fellow with whom I'd been battling for years, Harry Cohn. I knew he was a courageous man. I called him and, fortunately, he answered. There was a ticket girl sitting near me in the box office, and I glanced at what she was reading, a paperback book. I said to Harry, 'There's the greatest story I've found in my life. It's called'—I leaned over to read the title—*The Man I Killed*, and I want you to buy it and I'll make the picture for you for fifty thousand, if you'll send it to me in an hour.

"I got the fifty thousand within the hour, so I had to go and make this paperback novel, which didn't make much sense, into a movie. So we wrote a new story and called it 'The Lady from Shanghai.' I'd *intended* to make a B picture and then run out of town, but Harry Cohn persuaded me to do it with Rita Hayworth, who was then my wife, and it turned into an A picture, as well as an interesting picture, because it's still being shown."

It reminds me of the time when one of my largest entertainment contracts was sketched out on the back of a napkin in a lounge of Caesars Palace. Today, the majority of film studios are public corporations, and the echelons of executives the creative people deal with are more skilled in "business" than in "show." This is a reflection of our economic climate. It is a lively and continuing debate in Hollywood if the movie industry is better or worse off this way. I tend to admire the moguls of the past: Harry Cohn, Jack Warner, Darryl Zanuck, Louis B. Mayer, David Selznick, Sam Goldwyn. They came to films from other businesses, but they learned the movie business and operated more on instinct than on any other quality. But that is the one quality, above all others, that initiated the creation of so many memorable films. You got yes or no answers, and quickly. And as Jack Warner was to tell me, as long as his guesses were right fifty-one percent of the time, his studio made money.

"What I can't take nowadays," Orson says, reminiscing about the film studios, "are all the college graduate producers who live with words like 'creativity' and 'input.' It's much better to have Harry Cohn throw the telephone directory at you because he didn't like what you were doing. You knew where you stood. Harry Cohn once bugged my office when I worked for him. So when I came to work in the morning I'd play the theme song from my radio show on a gramophone and

I'd say, 'Good morning, this begins another day in the Orson Welles office . . . hope you like it!' At the end of the day I did a formal sign-off. But I enjoyed fighting with Harry Cohn, because you understood the terms of the fight and you respected a great showman."

What is lost as movie studios become large public corporations is the personal touch a studio used to imprint on its films. When a studio is simply a wing of a conglomerate, such as Paramount, which is owned by Gulf and Western, the people in power at the top are reading cash flow charts, not scripts. To be sure, without able people reading those cash flow charts, there is *no* money for any pictures to get made, but I don't think we'll be hearing in the future the kind of charming story Orson tells about Sam Goldwyn.

"I remember Sam Goldwyn on the set of 'Dead End.' It was based on a play, part of which took place in a New York slum, with a high-rise, expensive apartment house looking down on it. The set director had covered his set with garbage, making it look like an awful slum down by the East River. One day I caught Sam Goldwyn on the set, all alone, secretly picking up little pieces of the 'prop' garbage, trying to clean up the street a little bit, make it a little nicer. Behind his action was the spirit that he really wanted to make the best possible movie more than he wanted to make money. I won't say he *didn't* want to make lots of money. But all of those great moguls were *devoted* to movies. They were monsters, but monsters of their own special time."

One of the greats, according to Orson Welles, was Louis B. Mayer, who specialized in personal theatrics as vividly as did his biggest stars.

Orson recalls Mayer as "the biggest ham actor who ever lived in Hollywood. He was the master of the quick feint, with tears running down his cheeks, when he wanted to cut salaries. When things really got too tough he'd grab his heart and just fall into a dead faint. Three times he sent for me and offered me the old Irving Thalberg job. He wanted me to be head of production on the condition that I would never write, direct or act in a movie again. He said, 'I see you controlling these sons of bitches,' meaning the other moguls. I used to love to go see him just to *watch* the theatrics in his office.

"Then there was David Selznick. One of my favorite stories about David is when we used to go to his house every Sunday and play charades. And David couldn't bear to lose. He'd get *very* angry if he'd lose. So I began to organize the steady guests so that no matter how the teams were divided we would throw the game, and David would lose. This went on Sunday after Sunday, and the evenings always ended up with our genial host cursing us mercilessly, following us out to the parking area telling us what bastards we were. He was a bigger, more manic and monstrous ego-dizzy man than all the rest. But he was also a man of enormous gifts: a real producer."

With movies like "Citizen Kane," "The Lady from Shanghai" and "The Magnificent Ambersons" to his credit it would seem natural for Orson Welles to consider directing the most complicated and important task in films. But he has indicated to me that he holds acting and actors in singular awe.

"You see," he says, "I'm a nervous actor. I work awfully hard when I'm not on the set. I envy those people who can learn their lines in the car on the way to work. Everything comes hard to me in the movies. I have to *work* at acting. I'm not one of those facile people. I'm not a born movie actor, and you can't mistake one. He can't do *anything* wrong on screen. And I have to be awfully careful not to do all *kinds* of wrong things. It's funny, but I don't know what acting *is*; I don't know what charm is; I don't know what personality is. All those things are mysteries. I've been directing actors, as well as acting myself, since a little after the invention of the wheel, but I can't tell you what it *is*. My kind of acting is just plain old sweat. When you come out on the stage you leave in the dressing room the things which don't belong to that character you're playing. The actor cannot put anything on. If you do, you're faking. There has to be a little villainy in you to play Richard III. So to play Richard III you have to leave all the other elements of your own self in the dressing room. I would come out and give you just the particularly nasty side of my nature. But if I don't *have* that side, I can't play the part. What you reveal is what a sculptor reveals inside a block of marble. You can't lay something on, like makeup, and come out saying 'I'm Richard III.'

"It's as true of movie acting as it is of stage acting. There's no difference between movie and stage acting, it's the same thing. The difference is whether the camera *likes* you or not. If the camera likes you, you're in. It likes some actors, but not others."

I think Orson's point is well taken. Dick Haymes used to dazzle me on stage, but when I saw him in films I found no magic at all. When the camera went in close his eyes didn't flash the way Cagney's did. You can see the difference watching cable TV when they present a Broadway show, taped directly from the theater version; the acting seems broad and contrived, the timbre of the voices sounds too assertive. Conversely, I have the feeling a Gary Cooper, with subtleties loved by the camera, would have been lost working on a Broadway stage.

"I used to walk on the set and watch Gary Cooper," Orson told me, "before we'd meet for lunch. I'd watch him do a scene and think to myself, they'll have to shoot that again tomorrow, it's awful. Then you'd see the same scene on the screen and it was wonderful. He did nothing, but it was *something* kind of nothing. Then on the other side of it is Jimmy Cagney. I think he is one of the three or four greatest actors who ever appeared in front of a camera. And he played every single scene as though he were in a theater that held five thousand people, and he didn't want anybody in the gallery to miss it. Yet there wasn't one phony note he sounded. So there's no rule about it. There's no such thing as overacting as long as it is *true*. And Cagney never struck a false note, proving you don't *have* to be quieter in front of a camera. You only have to be quieter *if* you're in danger of being a phony."

*

FRANK CAPRA—Award-winning director, on Clark Gable: " 'It Happened One Night' " is the real Gable. He was never able to play that kind of character except in that one film. They had him playing these big, huff-and-puff he-man lovers, but he was not that kind of guy. He was a down-to-earth guy, he loved everything, he got down with the common people. He didn't want to play those big lover parts; he just wanted to play Clark Gable, the way he was in " 'It Happened One Night,' " and it's too bad they didn't let him keep up with that."

JACK WARNER
Last of the Moguls

THE LAST GREAT mogul was Jack Warner, who kept control of his studio until the late fifties. I was under contract to him between 1952 and 1954, and he took a liking to me because I was more of an entertainer than an actor. I think in his heart all he ever wanted to be was a performer. He lived the life movie fans imagined a mogul should live, with a mansion in Beverly Hills, which was the center for lavish parties, attended by all the screen greats of Hollywood. At these parties Warner liked to surround himself with the gifted and the glamorous, but he treated them more like employees than idols—probably because to him they *were* employees. Jack smiled and shook the hands of all the stars, but God help them if they did something he didn't like. When he gave a dinner party he went over the seating chart with his social secretary, and if someone sat down where they weren't supposed to, whether it was Elizabeth Taylor or a member of European royalty, he told them to move.

Warner's instinct was his guide, and he followed it ruthlessly, and with great success. "My brothers and I *created* the talking pictures you see today," he told me once, after I no longer worked for him. "There was no such thing as talking pictures, music or sound effects in film. That was 1926."

But Warner wanted his pictures to talk, even though the rest of the industry thought he was crazy: "So much so that quite a few of the men at the top companies said to me, 'You won't last ninety days.' *They* probably had some notes due in ninety days and thought we were going down with them. The reason they opposed us goes back to the life of Thomas Edison. He invented film, celluloid. He started to make a talking picture because of his other invention, the phonograph. But it failed, it didn't amplify the voice because there were no such *things* as amplifiers; this was around the turn of the century. He gave up talking pictures and everybody thought it would never happen. If a man like Edison couldn't make a voice come out of the screen, how could anyone else? And the industry didn't like it because it meant a whole new way of life for all the people in the making of films. It meant a complete revamping: studios, equipment, theaters, all over the world. It was a major step to try and take. We had been working undercover two or three years in the laboratory we had in Brooklyn, backed by a company called American Telephone. We chose Al Jolson and 'The Jazz Singer' for our debut. And it was a beginning of a new era."

Today major studios may release only a dozen films in an entire year. Under Jack Warner, his studio was producing over two hundred films annually. And therein lies his "percentage" theory mentioned earlier. "You are *lucky* if you can hit fifty-one percent. I aimed at that, and I believe that's about my batting average. If you hit fifty-one percent you are in business . . . forty-nine percent and you go broke."

With the cost of films now, that would be a risky percentage, unless you have a "Star Wars" or "E.T." on your list. In Warner's era a studio had the luxury of retaining a stable of stars whose name on a theater marquee guaranteed a picture would make money. There are no such guarantees today. A Clint Eastwood, Burt Reynolds or Robert Redford is going to sell a larger number of tickets, but with the cost of today's films, that might mean only a break-even situation. But in the thirties, forties and fifties Warner was in the position of *knowing* that Bette Davis's involvement in a film meant money for the studio. She made forty-six films under Jack Warner's management, and in his own words, "There were only three that didn't quite smash. The balance were all moneymakers."

*

BETTE DAVIS—On what happens when a demanding actress, like herself, meets a demanding director:

"Well, if the director stinks, the demanding actress becomes impossible. After all, it's your name up on the screen, and the public doesn't know as much about the director as they do about the star."

On the use of color in films: "Sometimes, the drama of a film goes when it's filmed in color. It gets pretty, too pretty."

*

Of the hundreds of films made under the eye of Jack Warner, his favorite is also my favorite—"Yankee Doodle Dandy," starring Jimmy Cagney. It was big without being silly, entertaining but not corny; since then Hollywood has had a hard time doing musicals, although films like "Funny Girl" and "The Sound of Music" certainly hit their mark. The discovery of Jimmy Cagney remained as one of Jack Warner's proudest moments.

"Jimmy was one of the greats. Some of them were on top when I engaged them, and some were not. Jimmy was a vaudeville actor in New York, working in a song and dance revue with two other guys. We happened to finance the show and found him in it. You see him now on the late show, and you can see *why* he was great; he knew what to do with his hands, his eyes, his whole body. There was movement, real excitement.

"Another great one was Edward G. Robinson. I happened to put him into a film, 'Little Caesar,' and there's a scene when he starts putting part of his thumb in the guy's eye that's just indelible.

"John Garfield was an unknown who came out here with us and did wonderfully. I remade a woman named Joan Crawford with 'Mildred Pierce' and she won the Academy Award.

"I brought Errol Flynn over from England. We had a studio twenty miles from London in those days. My studio manager said there was a handsome young man there playing a bank clerk in a film. I met Flynn, talked to him, brought him over here. I asked him how much he could live on, and I gave it to him in a long-term contract. However, I don't think his history is written on the screen, I'm awfully sorry to say. He was a great, great actor, and I am sorry the good Lord took him away as early as He did."

It is not exclusively the cost of films that has reduced the output of the major studios from twenty pictures a month to twelve a year. In the early years of the film industry most major studios owned chains of theaters across America, and were forced to create product to fill weekly double bills. Warner Brothers alone owned five hundred theaters, with another twenty-five hundred owned by other studios, but then the government brought antitrust legislation against the studios. Then, as Jack Warner told me, "We had to be either in the theater business or the production business, so everybody chose the motion picture end, and the theater thing went to pieces. You didn't have to make pictures for your own five hundred theaters, so we'd just sit and make the pictures, little by little, and in a matter of twenty years the whole thing deteriorated. At one time I was making seventy pictures every fifteen weeks. It got down to where I was lucky to make fifteen in all. You tried to make the things you felt would be a big hit. That's my opinion of what started the film business on the decline."

And so Jack Warner got out of the movie business, though he held on longer than the other great moguls. But they are men remembered fondly, if sometimes grudgingly, by those who worked with them.

FRANCIS FORD COPPOLA
The Riverboat Gambler

I spent all of my childhood Saturday afternoons in a movie theater, taking in the double feature, the Movietone News, and more often than not, watching the program all over again. When I struck out on the road with Freddy Martin and his band, doing hundreds of one nighters, one city after another, I spent the rare evening off in a movie theater, catching up on the latest releases. These days, it's a little tougher to get me out of my den, away from the videotape players and my ever-increasing library of films on tape, and drive downtown, park the car, sit through the cartoons and watch a new feature film. I suppose when you've seen an awful lot of movies, as I have, you either go to *all* the new ones or very few. But there is one contemporary director who will bring me to the theater every time—Francis Ford Coppola.

Francis is a dreamer and riverboat gambler and, above all, an artist. He comes out of the Orson Welles tradition of taking whatever cinematic, financial or political risks necessary to achieve the kind of film he wants to make. At a time when Columbia Pictures was being taken over by Coca-Cola and 20th Century-Fox was diverting its film profits into golf courses and ski resorts, Coppola started his own studio and dreamed of creating a home for directors, writers and actors, managed by someone who grew up with and loved films, rather than large public corporations that look upon a studio as a means to generate cash flow and tax write-offs. Most of Hollywood warned Coppola that he would lose millions, yet without the dreamers and gamblers like him, can studios do anything but repeat the past?

"When I was a kid," Coppola told me, "the movies I loved the best, and that made me love movies, were films like 'The Thief of Bagdad,' 'The Man Who Could Work Miracles' and 'The Shape of Things to Come,' all made by Alexander Korda. They were incredible, wonderful movies, full of integrity. Movies are such a tremendous influence on people, and the fact that someone will remember a phrase from a film, or a character will go to someone's heart, shows that films are a really important thing. Films should be made with that kind of quality in mind. Filmmaking is a game you should play with all your cards and all your dice, and whatever else you've got. Each time I make a movie I give everything I have; we should do everything we do that way."

Coppola's accomplishments are his best spokesman: Producer of "American Graffiti," "The Black Stallion" and "The Escape Artist," writer of "Patton" and "The Great Gatsby," co-writer and director of "The Godfather," writer and director of "The Godfather, Part II," "The Conversation," "Apocalypse Now" and "One from the Heart." Surrounding him is an aura of bigness: his films are *important,* made on the grand scale; he exudes the excitement attached to an artist who has the potential to deliver *the* movie at any moment. And again, the key ingredient is instinct.

"I think it's the same thing that makes you want to pick friends or lovers," Coppola told me, when I asked how he casts his films. "You pick them the way you pick people you want to keep in your life. Even though you don't have an actor in front of you all the time you think of their personalities. The actors that have an *effect* on me, or on the people I work with, are probably going to have a similar effect on an audience. When I was writing 'The Godfather' the studio wanted Ryan O'Neal or Robert Redford to play the part of Michael Corleone, because those actors had just made love stories that were successful, and the studio thought a Redford, or someone blond, would be a contrast to the Sicilian role. But I had met Al Pacino and this guy's face just never left me. When I was writing, particularly the scene where he is walking through the countryside in Sicily near the town his father came from, I kept seeing Pacino's face, and I couldn't see *anybody* else's. That made me keep going back to the studio to convince them to take Pacino. It's something you can't put your finger on."

On one of the occasions Coppola was at my studio, prior to a show, he sat in his dressing room with a large group of assistants, poring through photographs of actors as he pushed to cast his next film. An assistant thrust one photograph after another in his face, and he quickly judged them, using only facial expressions to let his assistants know how he felt. Even as our makeup man touched up his face and our wardrobe man straightened his tie, he was talking locations with his staff, making plans for the next day's schedule. I thought we were back in the days of the great moguls!

Al Pacino was not his only piece of offbeat casting for "The Godfather." Francis was just about the only one who was convinced Marlon Brando should play the lead role. At the time the film was made, Brando wasn't considered a box office name; and on a big budget movie like that one, studio executives sleep better knowing their film has a "turnstile" name in it. Coppola doesn't accept that theory.

"Anybody who has followed it has seen that if you go back and look at the big successes they haven't had stars in them.

Who was the star of 'American Graffiti'? It was the movie, and it was George Lucas who created it. Who was the star of 'Rocky'? An unknown. 'Star Wars'? 'Jaws'? You'll see that you don't need the so-called great stars. What the great star does has nothing to do with the audience or the making of the film. The star has to do with the banking philosophy of the studio— the star is the insurance that if it's a turkey at least they'll get *some* of the money back; it's a bottom line insurance.

"I thought Marlon Brando could play the part of the godfather. I had always idolized Marlon, ever since I was a theater student when my heroes were Tennessee Williams, Elia Kazan, Arthur Miller and Marlon Brando. So the thought of working with Marlon Brando was intoxicating. But the studio didn't think he should play the part. I called Marlon and literally trembled when he came on the phone—that's how impressed I was. I suggested, sort of obliquely, that I come over and we improvise a little scene, and maybe record it on videotape. And the tests were a great experience for me. Marlon is a great man. He is funny, playful, affectionate, brilliant, he likes to talk and think about very interesting things. Marlon has been around long enough, he did what he had to do, and now he lives his life and says and does what he pleases. He got the part."

The Vietnam war remains a mystifying and disturbing chapter in American history. We were not prepared to understand it. There were no Nazis and there wasn't a Pearl Harbor to clarify our participation. I think it was a period and event better examined by artists than historians, or at least better understood by the former. And I don't think anyone has dealt with the large issues of the Vietnam experience as Francis Coppola did in "Apocalypse Now." Like the majority of Americans, I viewed the war in its early stages as Us against

Them, America versus the encroachment of communism. Then in 1965 I made a trip to England and interviewed the philosopher and historian Lord Bertrand Russell, who began altering my perception of Vietnam. He told me about atrocities occurring in Indochina perpetrated by *our* side. I didn't believe him at first, but the stories eventually became headlines, and the whole ugly specter of the war sickened and confused me, as it did a good many other citizens.

*

LORD BERTRAND RUSSELL—Nobel Prize–winning philosopher, on America's involvement in Vietnam, 1966:
"They are fighting there in order that the rich may be richer. It's quite simple."

*

Coppola was also confused and disturbed by the war. "Apocalypse Now" was his response to his own reflections.

"I had some bad nights, and I was really frightened a lot of the time," he said, recalling his experience of making the film, "not so much over whether the bank was going to repossess me for going over budget, but whether I could make the film say what I wanted it to; I wanted the film to be an *answer*. I can't say that I knew all the answers to the questions when I was making the film, but I wanted the satisfaction that it would in some way throw light on the subject. When they look at Vietnam one hundred years from now, it will be an important part of our history, and many things that are going to change the world, and change *us*, stem from that experience. 'Apocalypse Now' was a very unusual movie; it's not a pat story of action adventure—the captain goes up the river and then

blows up "The Bridge on the River Kwai." It *uses* that kind
of story within a stronger kind of film, and tries to understand
some of the themes that stand behind the war. Not analyti-
cally, but emotionally. More and more, 'Apocalypse' becomes
like a dream, a nightmare in which you're dealing with scenes
of morality, good and evil, that all of us feel *something* about.

"All people inside their hearts have little murders that they
commit often; the other guy gets the raise that you didn't, and
you feel that horrible thing we've all felt. War is nothing more
but those murders given a place where they can actually happen. That's what the Vietnam war was to me. The real issue
was inside the human being; you can't talk about it politically
because three hundred years ago people had *their* set of politics, and the wars kept going on. So it has to have something
to do with the human soul rather than the politics of the day.
That's what I wanted 'Apocalypse Now' to be about. There are
professional Vietnam analysts, and I'm not in that class, I'm
just a movie director. But in that perspective I can tell you what
I think.

"The reason the war connected in a way with the very fiber
of our nation is that we were a country founded on the concept
of truth and honesty, we were straight guys; we are hardwork-
ing, inventive and straight. And the truth of the war is that the
events leading up to and during Vietnam were *not* straight.
We the people, I think, felt it. We all want the country to be
straight, to be what it says it is; we do not want hypocrisy.
'Apocalypse Now' was *about* hypocrisy. The plot starts when
a general calls a soldier in (Martin Sheen) and tells him he has
to find and murder an American colonel who has started a
strange cult way upriver. Now, I have no evidence that a
general sent a captain up a river in Vietnam to murder a
renegade colonel. But the symmetry of the idea, of a general
sending an assassin to kill a colonel because the colonel is a

murderer, is such a morality play that I thought it the perfect plot and metaphor to set in Vietnam.

"Now, from that point on in the movie, Vietnam is not like anything you've ever seen; it's totally crazy. But ask any veteran of the war what it was like, and he can't *verbally* express to you what it was like. That's what I tried to put on film."

To capture his vision of Vietnam on film, Francis spent a lot of money. The film, shot on location in the Philippines, required nearly a year to shoot, and the final tally for the project was one hundred million dollars. Almost any other director— George Lucas and Steven Spielberg would be the two exceptions—spending that amount of money would be considered irresponsible and the money unrecoverable. But as Coppola said, he wanted to make the film *he* wanted, and it cost plenty. "Apocalypse Now" started getting expensive from the first day of shooting. It began with what is now considered one of the greatest scenes ever staged and recorded on film: the helicopter attack on an enemy village.

"It was the first scene we attempted to shoot," Coppola told me. "I was very naive when I began the film, and I conceived this battle in which you have an armada of helicopters flying over this entire North Vietnamese village, and you see everything in one shot. A camera above the helicopters meant you saw the choppers, the people on the ground, fighting and terrible explosions. I thought that to see this in full view would be extraordinary. But when we went to actually do it, we didn't know *how*. We had our helicopters piloted by Filipinos who were scratching their heads trying to understand us. We had an Italian camera crew. We had real Vietnamese playing Vietnamese, with a few French sprinkled in, and we had an American and Filipino ground crew speaking without understanding. So here we are, trying to get these helicopters off the ground, there's ten tons of explosives, and all these Italians with walkie-talkies yelling to the South Vietnamese extras, who didn't understand one thing they were hearing. I stood back and looked at this activity and realized it is one thing to be a director and wave your hand and say boldly, 'We'll shoot the scene this way,' but that accomplishing it is quite another thing. So this was the scene we started the movie with and I was *already* over budget by three and a half million dollars."

And that was the moment when the gambler had to come out in Coppola. The artist within him was allowed to conceive and assemble the elements of his project. But finding himself almost four million dollars over budget on the first day of shooting must have been disorienting. The studio was screaming, and Coppola had only one alternative: "I guaranteed the budget." Meaning he staked the millions that he had made on "The Godfather" films against the success of "Apocalypse Now." His entire capital was mortgaged for the sake of his film.

*

ROCKY AOKI—Founder of Benihana Restaurants:
"Twenty-five million dollars to me is nothing. I really mean it. I'm still young. I want to try and make it in this country."

*

"I really love my house," Coppola told me, recalling the moment he knew he'd hung himself out on the laundry line. "When I thought that I might lose it, that someone else would buy it and I'd never get it back, that made me sad. But then I figured if the movie really bombed and I lost all my money, I'd borrow from George Lucas and *he'd* buy my house and hold it until I could go out and make another film. Because my wealth is not based on money—that is not my concept of wealth. Our wealth is not based on how much money we have, it's based on what we can *do*. So if I was to be wiped out financially, I'd *still* have some good ideas, I'd still want to make movies. I have worked on a lot of films and I have made a lot of films, and even the ones critics said were *not* successes became so years later like 'The Godfather, Part II.' Critics didn't say that was a great movie, they said it wasn't as good as the first. 'The Conversation' was not a particularly successful film, but it was a nice film. And they all made money."

But to gamble these profits on "Apocalypse Now" was an extraordinary move. It's hard for almost anyone to conceive of having fifteen or twenty-five million dollars to gamble with. Most people who have it aren't about to risk it all on one movie, particularly on one about an "unpopular" war.

I was incredulous when Francis told me about the financial arrangement of the film. When I think of the work I've done over my entire career, which has allowed me financial security, I really can't imagine risking it all on one bold move. Whether it was ego or integrity which forced Coppola's hand, he made the move.

"It doesn't happen the way it's reported by the press," Francis pointed out to me. "It's not that I go out and say 'I'm going to risk a lot of money.' What happens is that you are working in a film and the executives say to you, 'Look here, Francis, we've got to have the money by Monday, the bank won't put it up, you want to shut down or keep going?' So I tell them to put up the money and we'll figure it out later. Before you know it you owe millions of dollars. But you didn't *intend* to go out on a limb that way; you wanted to make the film, so you just kept going. And then the press says Coppola is a big risk taker. *I* never say that. On that level money is something so abstract. It's not like *my* money, it's just so abstract to me. They say, 'Do you want to keep working or do you want to stop?'

" 'Keep working,' I answer.

"Then three months later they tell me, 'You owe fourteen million dollars.' "

What separates Coppola from the average director, aside from the creative parts of filmmaking, is his attitude of responsibility that goes with his success. "I can go out and get a job and make in a year what most people don't even dream about earning in a lifetime. So it would be a sin for me *not* to risk what I had. To me it's not so amazing, and I'm surprised people are so surprised by it."

Because Coppola deals in megadollars and has been the force behind so many giant films, the press seems to treat him roughly. They love to write about his financial wheeling and dealing, sometimes with more fervor than is brought to the criticism of his films. He finished "Apocalypse Now," stayed around for its release, then went to Europe on a short trip. Upon his return he was greeted by distressing reports in Time magazine.

"I remember getting off the plane from Europe and opening Time and reading about my movie, 'This is the most disastrous film Hollywood has made in forty years.' How could you say it is the *worst* film in Hollywood in forty years? Whatever it might be, it was not that. As it turned out, it was one of the most successful films, financially, ever made. It's important that when an unusual new film comes out, that tries to do something in a new way, the critics don't *have* to say it's great or it's terrible. Not immediately. I think you have to say, 'I want to look, think about it, then see how I feel.' How can you write a review of a movie that someone worked on for one year, after seeing the screening, then rushing back to get the review to press in two hours?

"Look, I have things that I love the most in life which I didn't like when I first got them. People I thought were so handsome or beautiful, a week later they didn't seem so handsome or beautiful; other people I thought were plain, they really *were* beautiful. Things of quality you *live* with, and they get better and last longer. Whether they admit it or not, people in the movie business dream of making a classic, a film that will live, that people will look at in thirty years, that's considered a real work of art. And only time can really tell that. So when I make films I try to break new ground. At first it may be frightening, even repulsive, but I believe that after a while it becomes something you understand."

*

DON SEIGAL—Director of "Dirty Harry," on Clint East-
    wood:
"Even though Clint is the top box office star, I don't know if he is truly appreciated as an actor. He is really the Gary Cooper of today, and could be considered the John Wayne of today."

*

I remember watching Coppola on television the night his "One from the Heart" premiered at Radio City Music Hall. It was a public screening, rather than an opening for the press and celebrities. And for that very reason certain members of the film press were hostile; they didn't like being treated just like *any* moviegoer. One had the impression they were out to get Coppola. Like "Apocalypse Now," the film had gone over budget and Francis guaranteed the money out of his pocket, to the tune of fifteen million dollars. The Los Angeles press was covering the budgeting problems of his studio like the news staff was covering developing international crises. There were daily reports from the set. By the time the movie came out, the making of it was more of a story than the film itself. Once again, there was Francis Coppola, having spent a year preparing his film, facing a press corps that seemed, inexplicably to me, openly hostile. The movie was screened, the news cameras interviewed the first hundred people who exited the theater, then they all rushed backstage to where Coppola was holding a press conference. I watched it. He looked angry. When I saw him a couple of weeks later I asked him about it.

"Anybody would be angry," he said. "Here's a movie I worked on all this time, with so much hope and faith, and then a TV news unit waits outside the theater and the first ten people who come outside are asked how they like the picture. Then they rushed to the press conference and the first question is, 'How do you feel that nobody likes your film?' And I said simply, 'What do you mean?' And they answered, 'Six of ten people interviewed said they didn't like it.' But they *didn't* say that the people who did not like it are always the first out of the theater. The other people are in there clapping. It's not *fair*. I felt like I was in the 'Twilight Zone.'

"To criticize, to be a critic, is not to say *just* what's bad with a film, it really means to discuss it. It's a critic's job, as I see it, to discuss the picture, to wish it well, unless the motives or ethics behind its making are reprehensible. Generally, movies are hard work, and I do think we should wish the people who make them well, to root for films to get better, and to stress that when they do. Instead, I think a lot of film criticism really is more about the position of the critics, one to another, who is the top dog . . . if *he* says the picture is bad, the satellite critics assume the picture *is* bad, and anyone who says that it is good is going to look like a jerk. There is a hierarchy and pecking order among critics that's always shifting, like any profession, and it does not have anything to do with whether the specific movies are good or bad."

Well, you can say to any film director that you have to take the hard knocks along with the praise, but I think Coppola raises a point beyond the simple sensitivity of a filmmaker. I've been reviewed all my life. Every time I've stepped on a stage to sing, appeared on television with my show or even just given an interview to the press, I've been analyzed, criticized, *judged.* Sometimes favorably, sometimes not. But when you've frequently been in the position of having your work reviewed, and you sit back and read the clippings from around the country, you can see what Cappola is talking about. I remember a couple of years ago a major critic wrote a piece on the demise of the original-format talk shows, those shows based on the Jack Paar perception of what a talk show should be. And after that piece, other pieces trickled in, similar in form and content, from around the country. On the other hand, a major newspaper gave an early favorable review to something I'd done not long ago, and I saw the ripple effect across the country—good reviews poured in. It can be frustrating for a television host to spend weeks preparing for a certain interview or show, and then be criticized for some extraneous factor—the suit I wore, or the number of commercials in the show, rather than judged for the show's content. When I did one of the first interviews with Spiro Agnew after he resigned the vice-presidency, I was heavily criticized in the press, not for the content of the interview, which in the perspective of history turned out to be rather newsworthy, but for the simple fact of *presenting* him. Coppola is critical of the overnight judgments made by certain members of the media. When he spends a year putting all his expertise and heart and knowledge into a film, it is frustrating to be reviewed for financing the film himself, rather than its content. Not to stretch a point, but Michelangelo's Sistine Chapel was lambasted by many upon its completion, but the passage of time has proved its value. I truly believe we can't treat our great artists like Coppola with the People magazine flippancy we apply to a celebrity romance. It is a damaging trend in our culture to do so. And it affects the kind of film the public ultimately is allowed to choose from.

"Years ago films were allowed to be of many different types," Coppola contends. "There was the swashbuckler, the romantic historical, literally hundreds of different kinds of films to choose from. Today, what is allowed by management to be made, and approved by the critical establishment, has gotten so narrow that there are only four or five kinds of movies you *can* make. That's why the films, for a while, all seem to be about people in burning buildings, or they are all of another, common kind. We *need* a greater range of pictures so we can have more choice."

*

JOHN WAYNE—On westerns:
"The folklore of any country is the best understood thing about a country by others. People understand a little bit of the Irish from their folklore; we understand some other countries that way. And our folklore, the cowboy, represents one hundred years of legends in prose and poetry and song. Ours is about the most popular folklore in the world. So people want to see it, because folklore is about basic emotions; there's no nuance, people can just sit there and enjoy themselves."

On the roles he chose to play: "I like to play a character that a large number of people can identify with, whether it reminds them of their father, uncle, brother or whoever; I want the role to have human dignity. Cruel, tough and rough, that's all right; but never mean or petty."

*

ANDREW McLAGLEN——Director of five John Wayne movies, on Wayne as an actor:

"John Wayne was not a good actor, he was a *great* actor. One of the toughest things to do is to act yourself, act a natural character. And he knew how to do that, like Spencer Tracy, Clark Gable. They had a certain something that really wasn't acting, but is tougher than acting. You don't go to acting school to learn that."

VERY PUBLIC SERVICE

*

JULIE NIXON EISENHOWER:
"I would go for the Presidency, if I chose a political life,
because that's where you can do the most."

*

HENRY KISSINGER
The Man Who Made History

HENRY KISSINGER WAS angry.

This was April 1982, and an article in the Atlantic was about to hit the newsstands containing charges by former White House aides that Richard Nixon had once discussed with Kissinger the possibility of nuclear attack on the North Vietnamese, and that during the latter part of his Presidency, Nixon was often incoherent during meetings, distracted as he was by Watergate.

Henry Kissinger, former national security advisor and secretary of state, thought the charges were outrageous, ill documented and unfair.

It happened that he was booked to appear on my show a few days after the highlights of the inflammatory article had been leaked to the news media. This was to be the first opportunity for anyone to ask Kissinger about the charges. He told one of our talent coordinators that he didn't wish to talk about the Atlantic article, because he didn't want to boost its sales.

Our program is primarily entertainment, but over the years we have presented our share of controversy and newsworthy discussion. When I'm sitting opposite a guest of Kissinger's historical stature, I feel a journalistic responsibility to hit the issues the public wants to know about, and not allow the guest

167

to retreat behind a soft personality interview. So without mentioning the Atlantic article, I asked Kissinger a point-blank question: "Henry, did Nixon ever say during the conflict with North Vietnam, 'We may have to nuke them'?"

Kissinger was still recovering from heart surgery and he replied with much humor: "If you get too rough with me I'll probably just keel over, and the audience will blame *you*. But as to your question, you have to remember people were working eighteen hours a day under great pressure. I do not remember such a comment. It is not *impossible* that when the North Vietnamese, who really are the most obnoxious negotiators I've ever met, were being *particularly* obnoxious that [Nixon] may have said that. Anybody would know he didn't mean it. He never had a plan to use nuclear weapons [in Vietnam]. We never got *close* to using nuclear weapons. All of these characters who were working in the bowels [of the White House] and picking up phones now think they listened in to conversations, and thirteen years later give great interviews about it, but they just didn't understand what was going on. There was never any plan by the President to use nuclear weapons. And what he *might* have said in an idle moment . . . thirteen years after the event no one can remember. Even if it *were* said, it would never be said as an order."

Journalists have suggested that during the period of extraordinary emotional pressure Nixon experienced preceding his resignation it was Kissinger who was forced to make decisions of state on his own because it was nearly impossible for anyone to see the President.

"No, I didn't do it all on my own," Kissinger asserted. "He still made the final decisions. Obviously, he was more preoccupied than he otherwise would have been, and he ratified what was proposed to him more easily than he normally would. But there was no period when he was not giving the final orders."

"Were there ever times when he was incoherent and couldn't deal with you?" I asked, hitting the article's second major claim.

"No. That's one of the myths being put out. That's absolutely *not* correct."

An Associated Press reporter was standing in the back of the theater as Kissinger replied to my questions, and the moment the two key points of the Atlantic article had been answered, the reporter had his story. In the following day's New York *Times* I read the article that quoted me and quoted Kissinger. During the next few days, clippings from papers all over the country arrived in my office, all of them carrying the same Associated Press story.

We were all a little proud to have scooped the media.

"I think Nixon will go down in history," Kissinger went on to tell me, "as a strong President. I think he would have gone down as a President with major foreign policy accomplishments. He was decisive in crisis, he was courageous, and he was President during a major transformation of American foreign policy. Watergate was a disaster for the country, for him, and it was pointless."

Considering the Watergate question, it has always been incomprehensible to me how Nixon let the thing get so far out of hand (a matter I'll get into in more depth when I talk about Judge John Sirica). Kissinger gave this perspective to me:

"One of the big problems any President has is how to control the huge bureaucracy, particularly the one he inherits that may not feel excessively loyal toward him. In the case of Nixon, this was compounded by the fact that he could be very decisive, at least on paper; he could not bring himself to call somebody into his office and say, 'You do this or else.' He couldn't do it. He had a horror of face-to-face confrontations, so he transmitted all unpleasant orders through his assistants. Since I was often in disagreement with his cabinet members, they naturally thought that when I transmitted an order, either I had put Nixon up to it, or that if I had not even done that, that I was just giving them my idea. Nixon would set up elaborate channels to get around his own subordinates, instead of giving them a direct order. I think you have to say, historically, that this was Nixon's weak point."

Power is the theme of politics. And politics at its highest level, the White House, breeds an attitude of urgency and importance among the top people there; but as the power fades, sometimes abruptly, the feeling of power slowly recedes. For example, when Spiro Agnew first appeared on my show, shortly after his dismissal as vice-president, there were a lot of demands made by his representatives relating to the content of our interview, the air date, the time of day for the taping and the absence of a studio audience. These were conditions Agnew was used to controlling as a powerful politician. By the time of his second appearance, a couple of years later, Agnew had adjusted to his new life outside the inner sanctums of political power. He was relaxed, modest, cooperative and informal.

Henry Kissinger experienced a similar "decompression," even though he left office willingly and with an honorable record of service to the country. I happened to be in a private airplane with him about a year after he left office. We were returning to Southern California after an appearance at a charity dinner in Colorado. Kissinger was complaining to me that he had spent months completing the first volume of his White House memoirs, and he couldn't understand the time it took for the publisher to prepare the manuscript for publication. He was quite impatient about it.

"Relax, Henry," I said to him, "it takes a little bit longer when they have to carve it into stone." He took the quip with good humor, then suggested he would have to get used to subordinates not moving quite so quickly now that he was no longer close to the White House.

When the book was published, Kissinger accepted an invitation for an in-depth interview on my show. Like Agnew's first appearance, this one came with strings attached. Kissinger didn't want to appear before a studio audience, the taping session had to be held in the morning hours (instead of our usual 7 P.M. time), his security staff required a lengthy study of our facility and he wanted to be totally briefed by my staff on what areas I might focus on during the interview. When Kissinger arrived for our 10 A.M. taping, he became furious when he learned that his West Coast security aide had brought several relatives to watch the interview. There was much discussion, conducted behind closed doors in Kissinger's dressing room, whether these people would be allowed to remain. Finally, all the problems were ironed out and we got down to business.

Two years later we invited Kissinger back to the show to discuss the second installment of his memoirs. With major heart surgery behind him, he was much more relaxed about the process. There were no stipulations (other than not wanting to discuss the Atlantic article) attached to his appearance, and I thought it would now be appropriate to ask him what it's like for an individual to pass from one of the world's most important, complicated and powerful jobs and return to the less rarefied air of civilian life.

"There's no question," Henry readily admitted, "that when you leave office there is a decompression period. You are used to making decisions about events, and suddenly you're cut off from information, cut off from the ability to influence things. Then after a while, you realize also that you don't have to pick up the newspaper in the morning wondering who is coming after you now, or who leaked this or that. Also, at the end of the day, you no longer have to feel that heavy responsibility." He looked relieved just talking about it.

For historians to fully gauge the successes and failures of Kissinger's career in public service will require many years of perspective. But regardless of what that assessment becomes, I think he will remain an interesting figure in our history books. First of all, Kissinger was right out of that Eastern intellectual establishment that Nixon detested. Kissinger commented:

"When I was at Harvard as a full professor, opposition to Nixon was so much taken for granted that if anyone at a dinner party said a good word for Nixon, it would have been considered unbelievable, that person would have disqualified himself in the eyes of his peers. They didn't laugh at me when I went with the Nixon administration—they were *horrified*. In fact, the first time I saw Nixon and he offered me a job, I didn't even understand that he had done so, because that thought never would have occurred to me. Also, he had put it in his usual indirect way to avoid being refused. Finally, John Mitchell got it straightened out and Nixon managed to see me again and convey the fact that, indeed, he had offered me a job and what it was, neither of which I had previously perceived. I then consulted my colleagues. At that point they were more willing for me to go, because they liked the idea of having one of their own in Washington. What they didn't understand was that when you are assistant to the President your obligation is *to* the President, not to your Harvard colleagues. And they became more and more unhappy with me because I was carrying out Nixon's policies, rather than their own, even though their own were liberal-democratic in nature, a philosophy which had just lost the election. And I agreed with Nixon's policies. But

Nixon, closely as we worked together, always was suspicious that I really was emotionally still attached to some of my former friends. Which was partly true."

Kissinger's appointment to the administration was the fulfillment of an American dream, the immigrant coming to this country and achieving one of its most important offices. As I followed Kissinger in the press during his Washington ascendancy, I always detected an impatience on his part with protesters and critics of the government. So when I did get the opportunity to talk with him, I asked if his foreign roots affected how he looked on his service to his country.

He nodded agreement. "I was fifteen when I left Germany. I saw how a democracy can go towards a dictatorship almost without the country noticing it. I remember, when I was eight years old, we were in class and somebody came in and whispered in the teacher's ear that Hitler had been appointed chancellor. We didn't pay attention to the news, but it was an absolutely decisive event. After that there was a dictatorship, freedom of the press ended, and we saw the persecution of the Jewish people begin. So I saw something of the fragility of modern societies that native-born Americans, fortunately, never had to experience.

"It left a mark, a residue, in two ways. First, I have seen how fragile modern societies can be, therefore I am leery of those who take the imperfections in American society as an excuse to assault all our institutions and all our values. Second, I have a feeling for the importance of America to the rest of the world. When I was a kid, America was a magic country in which people could be free, where persecution was not possible. And even though I didn't know much about America, it was a symbol, and I don't want that symbol destroyed for other people.

"America is a much stronger society than the Germany in which I grew up, but the bitterness of the demonstrations protesting the Vietnam war, the name-calling, the attack on all values, the way people seemed to take comfort in calling their leaders war criminals . . . I saw the beginning of a process which, if people didn't become aware of, could become very dangerous for us."

That period of history, the years just before and after the Vietnam conflict, is particularly vivid in my mind. Like so many Americans in the early sixties, I assumed we were on the side of right, that we were the good guys. But as the war dragged on I became increasingly disenchanted with our involvement, and through the vantage point of my show I could feel the pulse of the citizenry changing with me.

In 1965 I heard of plenty of gung-ho talk on the show about us keeping the world safe for democracy, and the audience would applaud. But by 1967 activist actors like Robert Vaughn and Jane Fonda were challenging our position in Vietnam, and the audience was divided in their opinions. I can remember when Jane Fonda was loudly booed for calling Lyndon Johnson and Richard Nixon warmongers, but I've lived to see Jane become something of a national hero.

While the protesters were screaming, negotiations were beginning, at a tedious pace, to end the war. I asked Kissinger how the American peace demonstrations were viewed from the perspective of the Paris talks. Did they help or hurt? This was his answer:

"I believe that these massive demonstrations, these assaults on the credibility of the government, gravely weakened our negotiating position, because the North Vietnamese knew that all they had to do was induce a bad situation and the blame for it would fall on the American government, certainly not on them. We began practically every negotiation with Le Duc Tho, my opposite number at the negotiating table, reading me excerpts from the American domestic press, citing the massive demonstrations at home. I told him it was none of his business,

and we would have ten minutes of debate. On one occasion I
told him it was rather revolting to hear this from a representa-
tive of a country that didn't *permit* opposition to its own
government, and suggested he leave the exposition of these
things to those who understood such matters. That kept him
quiet for one session at least, but it didn't prevent him next
time from reading antiwar statements from United States sena-
tors and newspaper editorials, both of which undermined our
negotiating position."

During the Vietnam negotiations, we did many shows with
leading journalists, pacifists, military leaders, politicians, radi-
cals and activists, all of whom passionately discussed Vietnam.
And more than once, as I asked questions, I was troubled by
the thought that while we were debating young men were
dying. It got to the point where I almost didn't want to hear
one more opinion about the war, pro or con, because the daily
death tolls were becoming so oppressive. While we debated,
soldiers died.

"It's horrendous pressure," Kissinger commented about the
negotiations. "Yet on the other hand, there is an incongruity
between what goes on in the conference room and the conditions outside that are causing so much suffering; this is because
negotiations move into stages. Each stage then is settled relatively quickly, and then you get hung up on details that turn
partly into a test of endurance—who is willing to stick longer
to his position—and partly into a test of ingenuity—whether
you can come up with a formula that is fair to both sides.

"In the urgency to find a resolution, I don't think it's a good
idea to try to trick the other guy, outsmart him, because you've
got to deal with him again and again. So while this process of
searching for formulas is going on, the discussion can take some
pretty petty forms, which are out of keeping with the importance of the subject you are dealing with."

We all read about the lengthy debate at the beginning of the negotiations, about the size and shape of the negotiating *table*. The insensitivity of these men seemed incomprehensible to me. Kissinger suggested an explanation for it:

"That took four months, it happened just before I came in. It was a delaying action, but it was also a symbol. The issue for the South Vietnamese was that if they permitted the Communist South Vietnamese an equal position at the negotiating table, this would immediately undermine their own position as the legitimate government of South Vietnam. But of course from the outside it appears endlessly petty and frustrating."

By 1969 Americans in enormous numbers, I among them, were asking the government why we just didn't get the hell out of there. We were compounding disaster on disaster. Nixon took office on a platform of peace, and I challenged Kissinger to explain why it took years, and several thousand more lives, to extricate us.

"You have to remember," he explained, "we inherited a war in which there were five hundred fifty thousand Americans already engaged, one hundred thousand from other nations, plus one million South Vietnamese . . . we couldn't turn this off the way you turn off a television. The *way* we got out would affect American credibility around the world, and therefore the lives of other Americans in other crisis spots. In addition, of the sixteen thousand Americans who died during this administration, eleven thousand died in the first year, before anything we did could have made any difference. Nine thousand died the first six months after our coming to office. So the question becomes whether the four or five thousand lives that were spent while we were trying to get a settlement were excessive.

"It takes *years* to remove five hundred fifty thousand people, and for the United States to end the war, the terms presented to us by the North Vietnamese were that we would have to withdraw unconditionally, and that we would have to overthrow the government with which we were allied and put a

Communist government in its place. *Then* the Communist government would assure the safe withdrawal of Americans. Now, can you imagine having half a million Americans sitting in Vietnam under those terms? We estimated it would take sixteen to eighteen months to remove them, working under the good will of a Communist government that could hold our troops hostage at any moment. That's why we couldn't just stop the war immediately.

"If we had done so, the disgrace for the United States would have triggered a wave of uncertainty around the world. We had a situation in the Middle East which could have exploded at any moment; if people thought that we would not stick by our friends, we might have lost many more lives in the Middle East and elsewhere."

Our extensive negotiation process, aimed at attaining "peace with honor" and an orderly withdrawal from South Vietnam, was full of noble theory, but in practice the government of South Vietnam was totally run over by the Communists once we left. We could have pulled out four years earlier and netted the same result, I suggested.

"No," Dr. Kissinger insisted, "the takeover was *not* at the minute we withdrew. We withdrew in January 1973, at a time when President Nixon was at the height of his prestige; he had just won a tremendous electoral victory, and the American people could take some pride in having achieved, with great sacrifice, an honorable peace. There was no reason to suppose that the American people would not stand behind the peace in Vietnam, similar to the way they stood behind the peace in Korea. Within three months of this, however, Watergate disintegrated the position of President Nixon; nobody could have expected that. Congress legislated an end to all American military operations in and around Indochina. On top of that, they cut aid to Vietnam from two billion dollars in 1973 to one billion dollars in 1974, to seven hundred million in 1975. This was at a time when fuel prices were quadrupling. So we couldn't give aid to South Vietnam, its military forces ran down, they suffered tremendous casualties and in total violation of all agreements the North Vietnamese put nineteen of their twenty thousand divisions into South Vietnam and just overran the country. If this happened in Korea there would be a war; in Vietnam our hands were tied, so the thing collapsed because no peace treaty enforces itself. And the collapse was importantly the result of our domestic division."

Henry Kissinger is often described as one of the most clever negotiators ever to represent this country. Yet there is little mystery, he maintains, in his ability to negotiate.

"Normally," he explained to me, "negotiators think they should keep their cards very close to their chest, make a minimum of concessions, give up only a little bit at a time. The disadvantage is that if the other side knows this is what you are going to do, they play the same game, so there is never an end to the negotiations; and when you actually reach your final position, your opposite number doesn't know whether you might not have still another card you want to play. I generally had the tactic, which I admit is unusual, of having two basic aspects to my negotiation. One, I generally told my opposite number what I was after because we finally had to settle and in the end the settlement *had* to reflect something he wanted and I wanted. Secondly, after I would go through an initial sparring period to be sure I understood his position, I would make all our concessions at once, and go immediately from my opening position to very close to my final position. This put him somewhat at a disadvantage. I'd make a bigger concession than he had expected, but on the other hand he knew I would stick to it, so it put him in the position of making a big decision.

"Now, you can do that with everyone except the Soviets.

The Russians have this reputation for being geniuses in foreign policy negotiation. Well, when you see the Russian government in action it is a group of very elderly gentlemen who press on year after year. What they have is enormous persistence. When they adopt a policy, whether it's good or bad, they stick to it for years on end. Gromyko thinks nothing of coming up with a proposal and repeating this proposal, word for word, year after year. American negotiators get restless if they have to live with the same proposal for three months. So the Russian advantage, if there is one, is that they wear us down with our own impatience. And the Soviets feel they have to haggle, and if they don't haggle in a negotiation they aren't getting their money's worth. I recall one specific negotiation with the Russians involving money. If I had followed my usual procedure I would have gone to our final position right away, which was lower than the one they had asked to settle for. But knowing their mentality, I asked for a ridiculously high figure, and by the time we haggled our way down, I got ten million dollars more than we had actually been prepared to settle for."

During the period when Nixon was fatally weakened by Watergate, Kissinger was considered to be the most powerful man in our government. But that kind of power is often misunderstood by the public. I once asked Gerald Ford how it felt to wake up mornings in the White House, knowing you are the most powerful man on earth.

"What's funny," Ford observed, "is when you look at a President you marvel at the scope of his power, but once I became President I marveled at the limits of my power. I think that is a tribute to the checks and balances system our forefathers designed for our political system."

Kissinger had similar reflections. "I had a great deal of power, but the funny thing is that when you have it you are really more conscious of the things you *can't* do, rather than of the things you can. There are usually more things to be done than you can possibly hope to do. So what is in the forefront of your mind is an awareness of the obstacles to what you think needs to be done for the country. The satisfaction you get out of having great power is that you know that what you do will make a difference in the future; there are not many people who can say that what they do will really make a huge amount of difference twenty years from now; that's the cake you get out of it. Usually, however, you are much more conscious of the limits of your power than on the scope of it."

Kissinger looks back on the opening of China and his Middle East agreements as the most important work he participated in. "The importance," he points out, "of anything we initiated still depends on the manner and circumstances in which they will be pursued. You can't be sure what is permanent and what is not."

For the public servant the law of nature and the role of government, I'm sure, are both a blessing and a curse.

JUDGE JOHN SIRICA
With Justice for All

HENRY KISSINGER IS a permanent and prominent part of our public service history. There is another man whose name may fade from prominence as time passes, but whose decisions during a crisis of American history were as important domestically as Kissinger's were internationally. As Orson Welles points out, great events and times allow men to realize their own greatness, and a latent power becomes fully developed when the moment of highest duty calls. I think that will be the legacy of Judge John J. Sirica, the presiding judge in the Watergate trial.

I don't think the decisions of any judge in this century have been more written about, debated and reviewed than those of John J. Sirica. The fact that sixteen of eighteen of his decisions were sustained in the grueling appellate process indicates he was up to the task he was called upon to perform.

Naturally, every talk show wanted him as a guest, but Judge Sirica resisted the invitations for a long time. Finally, after two years of telephone calls from my staff, he agreed to appear on the show; what I didn't find out until later was that we had an ally living right in Judge Sirica's home. We were told that when the publisher of his memoirs presented the judge with a list of television shows requesting interviews, Sirica's daughter happened to be nearby, heard my name mentioned and told her father we had a good show and that he should appear on it. Her opinion meant something around that household, because the judge agreed to make his talk show debut on "The Merv Griffin Show."

First, a bit of negotiating remained to be conducted. We wanted to present the judge in a one-on-one with me, then bring out another guest, one who might be in a position to challenge some of the Watergate decisions. The prospects promised lively television. Our research department had been collecting articles by William F. Buckley, Jr., who was a friend of E. Howard Hunt and who had written extensively and critically of Judge Sirica. "As long as I can come out with Merv and make my points," Sirica told us, "then I'll be happy to answer any questions Mr. Buckley has."

We scheduled the taping in New York at the Vivian Beaumont Theater in Lincoln Center. I spent several days reading up on the Watergate trial, and the first question which occurred to me was whether or not Judge Sirica had any second thoughts about the case. A couple of years had passed; had his harsh attitude about the Watergate criminals mellowed?

"I would have done one thing differently," he said to me. "Remember when I refused to turn the tapes loose after the cover-up trial? They were played in the courtroom for about only a hundred fifty people. Millions would have loved to have heard them at the time. I didn't release them because I felt that the defendants—if the case were reversed on appeal and with all the publicity the tapes would have generated—wouldn't have been able to convene an unprejudiced jury. But since that time I have thought about it, and if the American people can ever hear those tapes [which we now can], and hear the conniving, the conspiring and the arrogance of these people, they would have no doubt whatsoever about the participation of all these people [in criminal activity], including the former President."

The second question I addressed to Judge Sirica was the same that most Americans asked themselves when the scandal broke wide open and the cover-up pointed directly to the Oval Office: Why didn't Nixon reveal it and put a stop to the whole thing before a cover-up became necessary? The turning point, Sirica explained, came on the tape of June 20, 1972:

"June 20th was three days after the break-in, which is really the beginning of the whole mess. I listened to that tape more than once. The June 20th tape sets forth a conversation between Mr. Haldeman and the President. Haldeman told him about the break-in, and apparently mentioned some of the people close to the administration who were involved.

"Now, I remembered what President Eisenhower did when Sherman Adams accepted a vicuna coat, causing a big fuss and holler. The President honestly and courageously said, 'You've got to go, you've got to give me your resignation immediately.' Which Adams did. And Nixon had taken some of the credit along the line for getting Adams out.

"If Mr. Nixon had had the integrity and honesty and character of President Eisenhower, he could have done the same thing [with Watergate]. Three days after the break-in at Democratic headquarters Nixon knew about it and knew some of the people involved. Why didn't he say to Haldeman, 'Look, Bob, I want the resignation of all these people by tonight, and I am going to ask for time on television tomorrow night and I'm going to tell the nation what happened.' He'd have gone out as one of the great Presidents of our history, because he *was* on solid ground in his foreign policy matters. But what did he do instead? He was so worried about McGovern beating him—McGovern didn't have a chance in the first place—that he allowed his aides to cover up, and they lied and created an atmosphere of arrogance . . . I was horrified. I was hoping, as

I listened to those tapes, that nothing would indicate that Mr. Nixon was actually in this mess."

But Nixon and his aides *were* hip-deep in a scandal. When it came time for sentencing, Sirica made his most controversial decisions, and was pretty rough on all involved. The President, of course, was pardoned by his successor, Gerald Ford.

"I know Mr. Ford," Sirica told me, "and I like him very much; he made a fine President. At the time, I thought the pardon was probably right, to get this thing behind us, to get the country going again. But I have changed my mind about that for these reasons: I had to send a former attorney general of the United States to jail, costing him his license to practice law. I had to impose sentence on Mr. Ehrlichman, who also lost *his* license. I had to sentence Mr. Haldeman, and I had to sentence Mr. Dean, also a member of the bar. And I got to thinking, from the letters I received as a result of the pardon, that a lot of people feel there are two standards of justice in this country: one for the man who rises high enough in influence and power and another for everyone else.

"There are still people who think Nixon got away with something. I think it would have been better for the country if the grand jury had felt it had enough evidence to indict Nixon—he was named as an unindicted co-conspirator. And if the Senate impeachment committee thought there was enough evidence to institute impeachment proceedings, it would have been better for the public to try the case, no matter if it took a year, two years or five years.

"If Nixon were indicted, it should have happened in our court—not necessarily by me—and he should have been made to go through the same process the rest of them did. This country is strong, this country can take anything. Our system *does* work the way the founding fathers intended it to work, and would have worked in connection with Mr. Nixon."

My staff reported that William F. Buckley, Jr., had watched

and listened to Judge Sirica from the green room, backstage at the Vivian Beaumont Theater. He sat on a couch, legs extended in front of him, hands pressed together and held against his chin. Certain statements made by Sirica caused Buckley to purse his lips, tilt his head back and shut his eyes for a few seconds; he was apparently making mental notes and preparing his rebuttal. Then, when I introduced him on the show, he shook the judge's hand, sat opposite him and presented his case, purposefully not looking at Sirica during the entire conversation.

"I have been critical of Judge Sirica," Buckley began, "for professional and, I have to confess, personal reasons. When I was in the CIA for nine months my boss was Howard Hunt, and I was the godfather to Hunt's three children. Two months after Watergate, his wife was killed in an airplane crash, and I woke up one morning to read in the paper that I was executor [of the will], even though I hadn't seen the Hunts in five years. Under the circumstances, I thought, for Mr. Hunt to get a sentence of eight years, given the fact that anybody in Washington who had never committed a crime would have got thirty days' suspended sentence for that crime, was a political act. I think that Judge Sirica was a prosecutor, not a judge, in this particular transaction."

There was scattered applause throughout the theater. I felt a wave of tension flowing between Buckley and Sirica. Experience has taught me to keep quiet in moments such as these, to let the principals meet head on, unmediated.

Buckley continued: "Subsequent efforts, especially in light of the Hunts' disintegrating family situation, to bring the attention of the attorney general to the fact that this man, who had never done anything except serve his country throughout his lifetime, was rotting away in a prison for something nobody else would have been sentenced to jail for, found a political White House that denied access to a petition of clemency to the attorney general. *That* wasn't Judge Sirica's fault, but what I am saying is that the crimes of Watergate didn't end that night. There was a sense in which there was an abuse of justice, and it continues right on over into the suggestion that everybody—which this audience applauded—should get identical justice. The reason we have a Constitution of the United States that says the President is permitted to grant clemency is because the people who wrote that instrument recognized that there *were* certain circumstances in which that right was authorized."

Judge Sirica waited until Buckley, and the audience, fell silent. He then leaned forward with furrowed brow and said firmly: "I would like to try and enlighten Mr. Buckley about one or two things. I have never had a forum like this to explain why I did certain things.

"I didn't think the sentences were outrageous because *other* people might have gotten lower and lighter sentences. Everything I did in this case, Mr. Buckley, from the beginning to the end of the trial, has been reviewed by the Court of Appeals and the Supreme Court, all the way through. Let me read you a few lines of what the Court of Appeals said . . ." Sirica opened a copy of his own book and turned to page ninety-one: "This sums up pretty much the thinking of the appellate court, and I think vindicates the position I took. Here is what the court says:

> The public interest in safeguarding a record from taint is particularly keen when the case involves the integrity of the nation's political system, as can fairly be said when persons in the campaign of one major political party use clandestine contributions to penetrate the internal process of the other, and is consequently a moment in both the daily press and history. Judge Sirica's palpable search for truth in such a trial

was not only permissible, it was in the highest tradition of his office as a federal judge.

"That," Judge Sirica concluded, "is my answer to all my critics."

Everyone in the theater applauded, except Mr. Buckley, who seemed unmoved by the quote.

"There is obviously a legal interest in the pursuit of truth," Buckley countered. "There is and has been considerable criticism by the American Bar Association and by the American Civil Liberties Union about the use of judicial discretion for the purpose of extracting truth by the application of unusual sentences. Now, the fact that [Judge Sirica] has been applauded by a liberal court for having been instrumental in bringing down Nixon is hardly surprising."

The judge pointed out that of the twenty thousand letters he'd received, many from lawyers and other judges, ninety percent applauded his handling of the trial.

"Listen," Buckley retorted, "you've got to start on the assumption that enshrined in the Constitution is a bill of limitations. For instance, if I could prove to you someone's guilt, and we could get the truth from somebody by torturing him, you would all agree that I wasn't licensed to do it. I consider an eight-year sentence for a two-bit crime a form of torture."

I felt I had to step in at this point. Having reviewed my notes on the case, I couldn't let Buckley's "two-bit" description of Hunt's crime pass unchallenged. Hunt had demanded hush money, blackmail actually, from the administration. Blackmail is not a two-bit crime.

"He demanded money to pay his lawyers," Buckley countered. "He went broke trying to keep his family together; he never succeeded in raising enough money to pay his lawyers. Certainly, if you understand yourself to be engaged in the country's business, which he understood himself to be—with twenty-five years in the CIA you can understand why—you are supposed to be protected if you get into trouble. By protection, he simply meant the assertion of what legal rights he had."

At the time of the plane crash that killed Mrs. Hunt, the press speculated about the nature of the accident.

"She was carrying part of that money [paid to keep Hunt quiet]" Buckley explained, "to Chicago to launder it, at least that is a reconstruction. As the executor, I was in charge of appointing an attorney to look after the legal interests of the estate, and the attorney satisfied himself that there was no skulduggery involved in that accident." He paused momentarily, then added: "Maybe I should have sent somebody to jail for eight years, until he changed his mind [about the crash] and told me different."

Sirica bristled at the remark. "Mr. Hunt was sent to jail for eight years. The minimum term was two and a half years; he made parole shortly after that, about thirty months, so he didn't *serve* eight years."

I asked the two men to sum up their positions, since we were nearly out of time.

"Here we have a judge," William Buckley began, "who is telling you how you should have equal justice, you should do the same thing to Nixon that you did to Mitchell and Dean. Why doesn't somebody ask the judge, why didn't you do the same thing to Howard Hunt that you'd have done to a fifty-year-old Italian peon who had never committed a crime in his life, if he had broken into an office without injuring anybody. Would you have given *him* two years and seven months in jail?"

Sirica's turn: "Mr. Buckley, every case is different on the facts, and I think if you were a judge you would find that out. But one of the things I considered in giving lighter sentences [such as for John Dean and Jeb Magruder), was the cooperation they gave the government. You always consider cooperation with the government as a factor in sentencing. I don't think Mr. Hunt truthfully cooperated with the government from the beginning. So I took all those things into consideration before I sentenced people. I have no apologies to offer."

Although Bill Buckley made some provocative and valid points, I remember leaving the theater that evening thinking that if all our courts were in the hands of judges with John Sirica's integrity and character, our Constitution and Bill of Rights will be preserved in the best traditions of this country. He had faced the ultimate challenge of public service with courage and ability, and this country is probably the better for it.

With Alfred Hitchcock

With Francis Ford Coppola

With Orson Welles

With Jimmy Stewart, Josh Logan and Rosalind Russell

With Henry Fonda and Josh Logan

With Alfred Hitchcock

With Jack Warner

With Gore Vidal

With William F. Buckley, Jr., Malcolm Forbes, William Loeb and Judge John J. Sirica

With Henry Kissinger and Armand Hammer

With William F. Buckley, Jr. and Judge John J. Sirica

With Ronald Reagan

With Francis Ford Coppola, Cindy Williams and Gene Hackman

With Orson Welles and Rona Barrett

With Alfred Hitchcock

With Norman Mailer

THE KENNEDYS
The Family Who Made Things Happen

POLITICIANS ARE MY least favorite interviews. The key elements of a good interview are spontaneity and genuineness, two qualities that are dangerous for politicians to exhibit in public with the vigilant press recording their every move and word. Politicians have the persistent fear of making offhand remarks that return to plague them on national news broadcasts. In private their personalities tend to be more candid and colorful, but the public persona of the politician is guarded, rehearsed and usually dull. That is why exceptions stand out in my mind.

The press tended to chide President Gerald R. Ford for being plain and lacking fire; he wasn't a good showman. Presidents usually are covered in the way Francis Ford Coppola described the coverage of major movies: a few top correspondents, say the New York *Times,* the Washington *Post* and CBS News, will run stories with a similar point of view, and the satellite papers and news stations will often adopt that same point of view. After that, the original point of view becomes gospel, an example being Ford's "habit" of bumping into things or tripping. Someone captures a funny picture of him slipping while disembarking an airplane, the photo is seen around the country, commented on and in short order the President is known as a klutz.

191

But sometimes the simplest and most obvious traits of a person are the hardest to see. I think Mr. Ford's character *was* his simplicity and genuineness. We're so conditioned to expect glossy, prepackaged exteriors in our Presidents that Ford's quiet, undramatic humanity took us by surprise.

I was seated near him and Betty at a charity dinner shortly after he left office. One of the speakers was a teenaged boy who had escaped from Vietnam when the South was being overrun by the Communists. His parents and six brothers and sisters didn't make it. He spoke that night about America, about what it meant to come to this place of freedom, and how he dreamed that his family might someday escape from Vietnam and be welcomed here as he was. The former President listened intently. When the boy spoke about what it meant to have this country accept him and other "boat people," Mr. Ford reached over and held Betty's hand, and when the boy talked about his dream of being reunited in this country with his family, Gerald Ford began to cry. His intent expression didn't change, but I noticed a few tears slide from his eyes. By the time the hall lights were brought up again, Mr. Ford had dabbed away the tears and resumed his genial demeanor, but it was a moment I didn't forget. I asked him about it the next day.

"That was a very emotional scene for me," he said, looking surprised that I'd noticed his reaction, since the room had been darkened during the boy's speech. "Here was this young man, who had six brothers and sisters, his parents still in Vietnam, and he had come here on his own as a thirteen-year-old. It occurred when the Vietcong drove all of the Americans out of the country. We had one hundred and twenty-five thousand of these Vietnamese who fled from the beaches and were picked up in boats. I'll never forget that, because there was some criticism in Congress when I said we ought to take them in. We had high unemployment, the economy was getting worse and there were some who said, 'How could you let one hundred and twenty-five thousand foreigners into this country when there aren't enough jobs for Americans?'

"Well, in the first place, out of the one hundred and twenty-five thousand, probably only twenty-five thousand were men and women who would work; and a lot of our people in the House and Senate seemed to have forgotten that virtually all of us come from foreign backgrounds. We are the product of this great country where immigrants have been welcomed over the years. I just got damned mad at the reaction of some of the people who wanted to close the curtain down on these Vietnamese."

It is not Gerald Ford's nature to give vague answers to specific questions, so after I discussed the matter of the Vietnamese refugees with him, I also asked him the question that had plagued his administration: Had there been a deal made, prior to Ford's assuming the Presidency, to guarantee Nixon a pardon?

"It was August 1, 1974," Mr. Ford recalled, "when Alexander Haig, Mr. Nixon's chief of staff, called me and asked for an immediate meeting. He came over that morning and told me the so-called 'smoking gun' tape was about to be released under court order, and that the situation in the White House was dissolving, and I should be prepared within a relatively short period of time to assume the Presidency. That shocked me, because I had been assured many times by President Nixon that he knew nothing about the break-in, and that he had no part in the cover-up. Generally, I automatically believe people, especially friends of mine. That afternoon Haig came back and said, 'The circumstances have worsened since this morning, and I want to bring you up to date. The President has several options in the opinion of his staff, and I want to lay them out to you.'

"The first option was that he could fight it through. This meant probable impeachment in the House, a hard fight in the

Senate and he would likely end up thrown out of office. Second, he could fight it through the first step and hope the House simply agreed on a vote of censure. Third, he could step aside under the Twenty-fifth Amendment, and I would have been acting President on a temporary basis. Another possibility discussed by the advisors was Nixon pardoning all the Watergate conspirators, including himself. And then the last option, as explained to me by Mr. Haig, was that Nixon would step down and I in return would agree to pardon him. There was no discussion of this between me and Mr. Haig. I simply listened. I told Haig not once, but twice, 'I'll have no part of any recommendation. I don't want any advice of counsel pertaining to our conversation. I'm going to stay out of it.'

"Now, people still say there was a deal. But that's absolutely untrue. And I actually went up and testified before the House Committee on the Judiciary—the first time in the history of this country that a President testified before a Congressional committee. I wanted to lay the cards out. I don't see how anybody could have any suspicions whatsoever."

Straight words from a straightforward man, and I would like to see more of his kind in office.

My interest in politics, at least from the platform of my show, peaked in the sixties. The American people, I sensed, felt close to the great political and social issues of that decade. At cocktail parties we argued about Vietnam, the draft, the inner cities, the space program and, in the wake of the two Kennedy assassinations, gun control. In the seventies cocktail party conversation, in Los Angeles at least, tended to be about real estate. People were shell-shocked, I suppose, from the sixties' activism, stunned by Watergate, and it was time to think about our own lives, worry about what we were going to do today and tomorrow, rather than what an entire nation was going to do with itself.

In the sixties celebrity guests often interjected political opinions on my show, and the studio audience reacted loudly, depending upon the guest's position. We had then a strong sense that, collectively, our opinions *did* carry weight and that we *could* change things for the better.

Speaking for myself, the political enthusiasm stemmed directly from the Kennedys. There was always a certain optimism and hope emanating from Jack and Bobby. And I truly believe our national political spirit hasn't yet recovered from the murder of Robert Kennedy in 1968. He certainly didn't speak for or have the backing of all Americans, but I noticed a particular look in the eyes of his supporters that I haven't seen since, a wide-eyed enthusiasm.

Each year I play in the Robert F. Kennedy charity tennis tournament in New York, organized by the irrepressible Ethel Kennedy, and from that experience I can report that the children of Bobby and Ted just may be the new generation of leaders for America. There are so many of them you almost need a spotter to keep all the names straight. But I've been impressed by their political awareness and keen interest in the policies of this country. Talking with them is like participating in a political "think tank" where everyone has the same last name.

"I think everybody in my family have been raised to think that my father and my uncle had some ideals and goals worth pursuing," Robert Kennedy, Jr., told me. "I think we're all going to chase after them, too. Not necessarily through politics. If we all went into politics it would be very confusing.

"Both my father and my mother," he continued, "tried to encourage us to accept certain goals or certain ideals. I think they did it with a system of encouragement more than hard discipline. I think we weren't that heavily disciplined. They used encouragement and love, basically."

It certainly worked in Bobby Junior's case. When I met him he had just completed a book about Judge Frank Johnson, the Federal judge from Alabama who in the early sixties made some of the most courageous and important civil rights decisions this country has ever seen. Bobby Junior's interest in the history and ideals of this country did not come by accident. He told me, "We were all encouraged to take an interest in both history and contemporary politics. On Sundays we had to write an historical essay or learn a poem to recite at dinner. During the week my father always told us war stories, mostly about the Revolution and the Civil War, which he was very good at telling. And then we all had to keep a diary of current events. We did it to please our parents *and* to compete among ourselves."

Robert Kennedy was a politician who boldly discussed the key issues of our time, offering specific plans and programs. Every politician talks about wiping out poverty and achieving peace, but Bobby addressed these issues eye-to-eye with me on my show. Looking at him I saw a sincerity missing in the eyes of more than a few politicians I've interviewed. Bobby Junior is familiar with his father's beliefs, and has done considerable thinking about the shaping of those beliefs and where they might have led us.

"He had a sheltered kind of childhood," Bobby Junior said about his father, "and as a result of that—though he had a childhood where he was encouraged to learn and accept new ideas—he was a unique politician in that he continued to grow throughout his lifetime. He'd see something that a lot of us would look at and accept—we'd say 'My, there's a ghetto, there's a starving child'—but he would look at these things in a different way. 'That's unacceptable,' he'd say. It was one of his favorite phrases."

Bobby Junior went on to consider what kind of President his father would have made:

"I'm not exactly sure what kind of material or tangible changes would have happened. I can think of specific issues he would have handled differently. But I think in a general way we would have seen more flexibility in our society. We'd be looking at things with certain new ideas in mind, rather than stale old ways of handling things that we've come to accept. That flexibility would really have done something for the way we've looked at everything, from foreign affairs to unemployment to small domestic problems. I think things really *would* have been different."

When historian Arthur Schlesinger's biography of the late senator appeared, I invited Schlesinger and two other noted Kennedy historians—Theodore White, author of *The Making of the President* series, and William Manchester, author of *The Death of a President,* for a discussion of the Kennedy magic. It was a rare gathering of three award-winning writers, all of whom knew the Kennedys better than any other living historians.

We started the session with a question about the highly publicized image of Bobby as ruthless, or at least someone who liked to convey that impression of himself. Arthur Schlesinger explained, "From all accounts, he was a very nice, sweet kid. I suppose by the time a seventh child comes along parents begin to take children as a matter of routine; so I think that Robert Kennedy, as he grew up, felt the dominating thing in his life was to win his father's approval and his father's loyalty. In the course of 'proving' himself to his father he developed a kind of exterior of toughness, tenacity and censoriousness. He tried in a way to model himself in some aspects on his father."

In fact, though Schlesinger was later to be part of John

Kennedy's White House team and a confidant of Bobby, he didn't like him at first. "My first experience with Robert Kennedy," he told me, "was an altercation, as with many people who met him for the first time; one was put off by his seriousness. He wrote a letter to the New York *Times* attacking a policy set by Franklin Roosevelt. Being a great admirer of Roosevelt, I wrote a testy letter setting Robert Kennedy straight on that matter, which the *Times* also published. Bobby then sent a rejoinder to my letter, which the *Times* did not publish. So he sent it to me with a covering letter saying that when I had read *his* rejoinder he was sure I would then wish to write the *Times* and apologize for what I had said. John Kennedy, then a senator from Massachusetts, came to Cambridge about then and said to me, 'My sisters are very mad at you because of what you write about Bobby.' But he seemed very amused by the whole thing.

"So when I first met Bobby in the Stevenson campaign of 1956 we glared at and avoided each other as much as possible. At one point in the campaign we were marooned during a rainstorm in Morgantown, West Virginia, and we were forced to take buses to our next stop, Pittsburgh. We all ran through the pelting storm to get on the bus, which was dark, and scrambled for seats. I turned to see who I was sitting next to. It was Robert Kennedy. We were both filled with dismay at this discovery, since we were facing a four-hour bus ride. We had no alternative but to begin a discussion, and I found him extremely engaging, amusing, intelligent, and at that moment we became friends and remained friends thereafter."

As he grew to know Bobby, Schlesinger developed an understanding over the years of the "ruthless" image.

"He came from that Irish-Catholic family. In Protestant families all the brothers and sisters regard themselves as equals and all go off in different directions. Catholic families, Irish in particular, are a much more corporate family unit, like a clan.

Younger brothers and sisters all think it the most natural thing to serve the head of the family. Robert adored and admired his brother John more than anyone he'd ever known, so it wasn't a distortion of his character to serve his brother. And in serving his brother he didn't give a damn about himself. Running Jack Kennedy's campaign confirmed this impression of 'ruthlessness.' "

Who fostered the ruthless label, according to Teddy White, is an important question to ask. White told me: "A man should be respected for the enemies he makes. Robert Kennedy made *good* enemies: the teamster racketeers, the racists and bigots, the ignoramuses. He made good enemies, and though I loved him for himself and his family, I *respected* him for his enemies."

Teddy White was covering Bobby's 1968 Presidential primary campaign, and has a particularly poignant last memory of him: "When I hear these stories about the 'ruthless' Bobby Kennedy I think of the last two days of his life. I'd been on the campaign with him for six weeks and I was exhausted; Bobby could just wear you out. So on Monday I couldn't get out of bed. Bobby was going out to campaign and he came first into my room, stuck his head through the doorway, and said, 'Chicken!'

" 'Bobby,' I said, 'I'm too sick, you've worn me out.'

" 'Okay,' he said, 'I'll report to *you* today. I'll come back this evening and tell you what happened on the campaign, and you can write it all up in bed.'

"I told him it was a marvelous suggestion, and he said what I had to do in return was arrange a beach date for his kids the next day. *That* was the 'ruthless' Bobby Kennedy, telling an ailing campaign reporter to stay in bed, he'd take care of the reporting.

"He was dead twenty-four hours later."

Had the tragedy in Los Angeles not occurred, and had

Bobby gone on to win the nomination of his party and, finally, the election against Richard Nixon, history would have changed dramatically, according to Arthur Schlesinger. "Had he been elected, I believe we would have pulled out of Vietnam in 1969 rather than 1972, which means that a lot of Americans and a lot more Vietnamese who are dead would still be alive. I think we would have seen a much more direct attack on the decay of the cities in America and on the problems of the poor and powerless in this country."

The Kennedys are America's version of a royal family, and like England's House of Windsor much myth has been entwined with the facts of their history. I asked William Manchester and Teddy White to offer some perspective on the Kennedy charisma that has engendered such public interest.

"In the first place," William Manchester explained, "they were and are physically attractive people. They're very energetic, bright, imaginative and idealistic; they're always well informed. Certain people have private and public roles which are played quite differently from each other. For example, Adlai Stevenson in private was very different from Adlai Stevenson in public. In fact, the only public person I've known who was the same man with me as he was in front of an audience was Winston Churchill; he addressed me as if I was a one-man House of Commons. But John Kennedy was far more effective in private than in public. He is known to have been a fine public speaker, but I found him in conversation to be so quick, so sharp and so well read that it was rather intimidating. And he had a way, as I think all the Kennedys have a way, of involving you in their decisions, asking what *you* think they should do.

"Robert Kennedy was the same way. I remember sitting at the pool at his home in Hickory Hill in the spring of 1964.

Bobby said he was thinking of running in New York for the Senate, and asked what *I* thought. I said, 'You'll never make it there, run for governor of Massachusetts.' That was typical of my political wisdom. But he was actually asking *me* what he should do, and that's very flattering *and* very effective."

We remember them so vividly, Teddy White asserted, simply because they indeed caused a change in our lives.

"These people made things *happen,*" Teddy said. "It was a generational jump John Kennedy took into the White House. He followed Eisenhower, our oldest President. JFK was of the generation that actually *fought* World War II, the generation that held the guns. This country charged out of the 1930s with John Kennedy. Our generation took over with him in 1960, and nothing more eloquent could have been spoken than his inaugural address. I don't want to create mythology about him, but the Civil Rights Act of 1963 is such a *magnificent* act; the economic organization of our country in 1963 is again an act of magnificence. He made his mistakes, he had his faults, but he was a great President. If there is a myth about him, I suppose we are all responsible, because this man had not only charm but also elegance. And he was a lot of fun to be with. There was something in him that made us look beyond tomorrow to the *far* tomorrow.

"He wasn't afraid to assume his responsibilities. On a big decision, like the Bay of Pigs, which was a mistake, or the Cuban missile crisis, in which he was beautiful, he would say simply, 'That's what I get paid for.' I can't remember anything more wonderful than John Kennedy's last off-the-cuff speech at the Boston Garden the night before he was elected President. I won't quote it exactly, but I'll give you a few lines. He said, 'I run for the Presidency of the United States of America after fourteen years in the Congress not because it is an easy job. I run for the Presidency because I believe it is the chief duty and central action of the President to put before the

American people the unfinished public business of our time.'

"I submit to you," Teddy White concluded, "a President can't do better than that."

John Kennedy's innaugural speech, as Teddy White suggests, will long be remembered. The phrase, 'Ask not what your country can do for you, but what you can do for your country,' is forever associated with the late President. When I met Evelyn Lincoln, John Kennedy's White House secretary, in the middle sixties, I asked her if Kennedy did, indeed, write those words himself.

"We were flying from Washington to Palm Beach, and he said he had some dictation to give me," Miss Lincoln recalled. "I noticed he had several yellow pieces of paper he had written notes on, and I thought he wanted me to answer some of his mail. But as he began dictating to me, all of a sudden it dawned on me that this was really *something*. And then that one phrase, 'Ask not what your country can do for you, but what you can do for your country,' came up, and I knew what I was hearing was historical."

Evelyn Lincoln went on to tell me that the President-elect spent a great deal of time learning and practicing that speech, right up to the morning of the inauguration. "On January 19 there was a lot of snow in Washington, which meant I couldn't get home. So I stayed the night in the Senator's home. I was keeping his copy of the inaugural address, and when I went to bed that night I thought it should really be locked in a safe. But there wasn't one, so I slept with it right next to me on the bed. In the morning I heard a knock at my door and there was Senator Kennedy asking, 'Miss Lincoln, where is my address?' I got up and handed it to him, and shortly thereafter I heard his voice coming from a bathroom down the hall. He was busy reading the speech aloud as he took a bath. A bit later he went into his room to dress and the speech continued. Finally, he came down to the living room, where breakfast was being served, and he was *still* reading his speech while he ate his breakfast. He *was* prepared."

I asked the President's secretary if she had a favorite image of him, a lasting picture. She recalled a moment from the election night.

"As it started out, the returns were very favorable for Senator Kennedy, but as the evening wore on, it became closer and closer. We were all gathered at Robert Kennedy's house, watching the returns on television. Midnight, one, two o'clock. The senator was relaxed, walking from room to room and chatting. At three o'clock he said he was going home to bed. The returns were still very close. I left with Ted Sorensen, who was driving me back to my hotel. We went out through the backyard and I looked at the house where Senator Kennedy was staying. And through a window I saw him, sitting in a chair, quietly reading a book. And at that moment I thought, 'I know he's going to be President, because he's confident.' He was already studying to see what he could do *after* he took office. It was the most touching picture."

Exactly what he and his brother Robert *could* have done provides moments of contemplation for many, and some tears.

NEWSMAKERS

*

SOPHIA LOREN:
"I think that human relationships have decayed, really, in a terrible way. Respect is a word that has no sense anymore. I have two young children, and I'm afraid for them, for what they are going to be facing in the future, and I hope that the world is going to change a little bit for our children."

*

BARBARA WALTERS
Asking the Right Questions

ON ANY NEWSCAST, whether national or local, you'll find a mixture of male and female correspondents. Women have Barbara Walters to thank for that. Like Billie Jean King in tennis, Barbara opened the door for women to command the same big dollars and prime-time exposure that men enjoyed for years. And like all pioneers, she suffered bruises while blazing the trail.

After working as a host of the NBC "Today" show for thirteen years, Barbara moved to ABC, with a reported salary of one million dollars a year. The press constantly wrote about her as "the million-dollar girl," and rarely with kind intent. I've interviewed Barbara over the years, and have always found her intelligent, amusing and conscientious about her work. I asked her once if she felt she'd been treated like the successful and accomplished professional newswoman she is.

"When I left NBC," she said, "there was a lot of strange publicity. They were very bitter. A lot of things were said that simply were lies. One of them was that I was a 'prima donna,' that I had made lots of demands for hairdressers, makeup, limousines. In fact, I was reading an interview in TV Guide with Walter Cronkite, who is a professional competitor and personal friend. He was talking about standing in the street while it was snowing and he said, 'If I were Barbara Walters I'd have a limousine.' That's how far things got. But I do *not* have a limousine. I walk through the park, or take a taxi or I take buses. I used to take the bus all the time home from NBC. It was the easiest way. What bothers me is this whole image. If Walter Cronkite got out of a limousine, or Tom Brokaw, okay, fine. But if I do, it's 'prima donna.'

"I read that when I went to China I took a hairdresser along. So I began, almost on purpose, to pull my hair back on trips —because I do my own hair—and let it get dirty to counteract the reputation that has been following me for three years. There's jealousy in every industry. There's a lady television critic in New York who, if I've just interviewed Sadat and Begin, would start out her article, 'Barbara Walters, who earns a million dollars and isn't worth it, has just interviewed Sadat and Begin . . .' I think that haunts you.

"When this kind of criticism hit in the beginning I cried, silently. And I think that's what saved me. I didn't cry on the air and I didn't whine. Now I don't bleed as much as I did. I look at the critics and think, 'for heaven's sake, this is just a critic, I'm as good as *he* is, or *she* is, so why let them destroy me.' And I think the only thing you can do in my position is continue to do your work and do it as well as you can."

I think one of the problems Barbara faces as a newswoman is that she does celebrity interviews. Critics are often uncomfortable if a television personality is capable of more than one enterprise. Barbara interviewed the late Anwar Sadat, Jimmy Carter and King Hussein, but she also interviews Clint Eastwood and Bo Derek. But Barbara Walters comes out of a journalistic background, and earned her stripes as a television journalist long before most of her critics.

"I never expected to have a life in front of the camera," she contends. "When I graduated from college, television was well underway. And I wrote. That's how I began. The idea of walking out in front of an audience wasn't in my repertoire, even though I came in contact with that sort of thing from my father at a very young age. My father was what you might today call an entrepreneur. He opened a nightclub in Boston called the Latin Quarter when I was young, then he opened one in Florida and then New York. My dad was a great showman; he cared about the shows, and presented these marvelous attractions surrounded by six-foot-tall showgirls. It was a strange life for a child, but a good life. You always hear about the minister's daughter who is a hell raiser; well, I never smoked and I don't drink. My mother is a nice, conservative lady. And in fact my dad was a very bookish man who loved to write and was very shy, not what you'd expect from a nightclub owner.

"I remember thinking I had all the pull if I wanted to become an actress, because my dad would be able to help me. I had pull, but no push. If I'd gone out and tried for a role and somebody turned me down, said I wasn't right, then I would have been miserable. But what I'm doing now is an entirely different thing, asking questions and writing."

And ask questions she does, of some of the world's most celebrated people. People in the news business and show business (and the two worlds are often easily confused) envy Barbara Walters's ability to land those major interviews with world figures, whether it be a head of state or Katharine Hepburn. But those people just don't come to her and ask to be interviewed.

"I wasn't born with silver contacts in my mouth," she asserts. "I work very hard. I call. I nag. I 'noodge.' Some of the big newsmen have their producers make the calls; they have big staffs and so forth. But right from the beginning I went after people myself. It was the only way I could get major interviews. In the early days of the "Today" show, unless I got an interview myself—meaning I went out on location and filmed it—I wouldn't get it, period. If an important person came into the studio, he was always interviewed by the man; I would never get a crack at it. Today that's changed. But that's how I began to get noticed, going after people and doing it myself. The first one was Dean Rusk, then later Henry Kissinger. To this day if I want to interview somebody I'll make the calls and pursue it. When we were trying to get Sadat in Cairo, I literally stood outside the palace and handed notes in, hoping that he would do an interview.

"Sometimes I'm simply forced to be persistent. I'll give you an example. Remember when Sadat took the plane from Egypt to Israel for that now historic trip? Well, Walter Cronkite arranged to be on that plane, which was brilliant. I don't know how it was done, but he did it. I arrived in Tel Aviv and immediately Roone Arledge, my boss, called and said, 'Walter Cronkite is in Egypt, *now.* He's getting himself on that plane. John Chancellor is going there, too. You get your fanny on that plane!'

"So I stayed up all night calling to try and arrange to be on that plane. You could not call directly from Israel to Egypt, so I was calling New York and working through intermediaries. Finally, without going through all the details, I got permission to be on that plane. I fly to Egypt and now Cronkite, Chancellor and I are on that plane. The plane takes off and goes to Ismailia to pick up President Sadat. We landed there on a dark, cold, starry night. Out of the darkness comes a helicopter carrying Sadat. Members of his cabinet are chanting in Arabic, 'Go with God.' Walter Cronkite walks up to Sadat, puts out his microphone to get his immortal words, and I'm right there with him. Sadat looks at me and says, 'Ah, Barbara, so you made the plane!' And then he said to Walter, 'So Walter, how do you feel about Barbara being here?' And Walter smiled and replied, 'It's not what I had in mind.' So that was Sadat's historic first conversation before boarding the plane for the famous trip."

That trip led to the interview that Barbara remembers as her proudest moment as a journalist.

"Yes, I'm most proud of the first interview Begin and Sadat ever did together, which was right after Sadat's trip to Jerusalem. I'm proudest of it because for years all of us had tried not only to get an Israeli and an Egyptian to sit down together, which was impossible, and the fact that we were the first ones to have them on that historic day, that's important to me.

"It came about like this. When I got on the plane with Chancellor, Cronkite and the presidential party, I knew that if I asked Sadat for an interview in front of Walter and John, it would occur to them that maybe this was the thing to do. So I sent a letter to Sadat's top aide and requested an interview with Sadat, together with Prime Minister Begin, or separately, whichever. When I got off the plane I had an answer: he would do the interview, alone. He had no intention of doing an interview with Begin as he stepped off the plane. But that Saturday night he was very euphoric, and so was Begin, who was very up. I did an interview with Begin that night and he talked so much and was so awake that finally—he had a big speech scheduled in front of the Knesset the next morning—his secretary said to him, 'Mr. Prime Minister, for the good of the country, go to bed.' Later that night Begin said to me, 'Barbara, I asked President Sadat if he would do the interview together with me, for history and for our friend, Barbara. And he said yes.' So that's how the interview finally came about, Begin arranged it for me."

The other famous Barbara Walters interview was with Fidel Castro. Certain newspaper columnists even speculated that Barbara was having an affair with the Communist leader. When the stories appeared it occurred to me that it wasn't likely the press would speculate that Mike Wallace was having an affair with Margaret Thatcher, if he happened to land an interview with her. But Barbara got the full treatment from the gossip press. I was doing shows from New York shortly after Barbara's return from Cuba, so I invited her to discuss the trip. And I gave her a "Barbara Walters" question right off the bat.

"Are you having an affair with Fidel Castro," I said, and watched as her initial surprised look settled into shock. Then she realized I was kidding. "If you asked that of Chancellor or Cronkite, you'd get popped!

"Actually, Castro bends over backwards to treat men and women just the same. Before going down there I read reports about how macho he is and how he flirts with all the female reporters; it's baloney. He treated me as a professional. He is very straight, has a very good sense of humor, but usually is quite serious. The only time he was uncomfortable with me was when I behaved somewhat 'female.' My production team had spent four or five days with him, and as we were leaving he shook my hand and thanked me for coming to Cuba. And I said this is how we do it in our country, and I bent over to kiss him on the cheek and he became very formal.

"We taped five hours of interviews with him, one hour of which aired in America. They played all five hours on Cuban television, except for one question. In the course of the interview I asked him if he was married, and why this whole aura of mystery with him about women? He got very annoyed and said, 'Why are you asking me that?' I asked him what the big deal was: it's a very simple question, are you married? 'Formally, no,' he finally said. When they played the show in Cuba, that one question and response were cut out."

Even Fidel Castro, Barbara later told, should be allowed to have a few secrets.

DAN RATHER
A Reporter's View of the News

"THERE IS NO question that Walter Cronkite is a star. He is also a reporter. Most of us in the business would prefer to be known by the title 'reporter'; some prefer the word 'journalist.' But either reporter or journalist is preferred to 'star.' " So said Dan Rather a few years ago, when he was the CBS Evening News "star-reporter-journalist" and heir apparent to Walter Cronkite.

When talking with Dan I felt reassured that our network news was in the hands of a professional, a man who in years to come would maintain the standards of integrity set by Mr. Cronkite. For the power of that chair and that platform is immense. On the CBS Evening News Walter Cronkite was anchorman *and* managing editor; he had a lot to say about what we heard in our living rooms. Dan Rather also has a strong voice in the choice news he presents. With that power in mind, I asked if a network anchorman could ever gain the power of, say, a Peter Finch in the movie "Network," in which the newsman assumed a messiah image in an effort to "save" the country.

"I think it's farfetched," Dan replied, "but, yes, it *could* happen. It would never happen with a Walter Cronkite, however. Among other things, Cronkite has taken the advice of the late Adlai Stevenson, who was asked about fame and celebrity; the advice was that the stuff's all right if you don't inhale.

"Walter always preached that to his subordinates. Television depends on the integrity of the people running it, just as with government. Bill Paley, the chairman of the board of CBS and one of the architects of television, isn't going to let what occurred in 'Network' happen. The people after Paley in the chain of command aren't going to let it happen. But the potential for that kind of thing is there.

"While I was watching 'Network,' in the back of my mind were memories of station KSAM in Huntsville, Texas, a 250-watt station. In the business we call it a 'tea kettle station,' where one man not only owns the radio station and operates it, but also does the newscast, the disc jockeying and everything else. In the case of KSAM it was Pastor Ted Lott. He hired me at forty cents an hour to run the station. And something happened apropos of 'Network' and of the importance of who is controlling the medium. This man Lott was a preacher; he wanted to preach Saturdays and Sundays, so he hired me to run everything at the station. I didn't even have time to eat. I opened the station at five in the morning and carried on until midnight. The second week I worked there I told Pastor Lott that, though I wasn't unappreciative of the job, I did have one problem. I worked around the clock and didn't have time to eat. So we worked on the following arrangement: every Saturday and Sunday at 6 P.M. I was to put on a long-playing record, hop into the KSAM mobile unit, which was a 1937 pickup truck, get myself down to the local dairy bar, pick up two burgers and a shake and get back to the station before the long-playing record was over. The very first weekend we tried it, this particular program featured Pastor Lott's itinerant preacher brother from Del Rio, Texas, who did a little guitar plucking and quoted a little Scripture. I put the record on, hopped into the truck and raced down to the dairy bar, where there was a new girl working I hadn't had the opportunity to get acquainted with. So I said to myself, it doesn't make any difference whether I eat the hamburgers here or take them back to the station, as long as I get back before the half-hour is up.

"So I decided to stay there, and she and I would chat and listen to the diesel trucks go by on Highway 75. I'd been there twenty minutes when the phone rang. The girl put her hand over the mouthpiece and said it was Pastor Lott, and he was not in a very minsterial frame of mind. I got on the phone, and it was indeed Pastor Lott, talking through his teeth. He said, 'Rather, have you heard our station any time in the last twenty minutes?' I told a little white lie and said there was a long line at the hamburger stand; I was just leaving. He said, 'You get back to the mobile unit, listen to the station, get *back* to the station, fix it, and then you are fired!' Click. End of conversation. I went out to the truck, turned on the station, and there was Pastor Lott's brother saying, 'Go to hell . . . go to hell . . . go to hell.'

"So, in that sense, the future of television depends largely on who's minding the store."

I'm an avid watcher of television, but I'll admit to an awful lot of channel changing, particularly with the eleven o'clock news. And I can't say I'm impressed with what I see. The news broadcasts seem to be turning more in the direction of supermarket tabloids than serious, unsensationalized reporting. When you watch the eleven o'clock news on a regular basis you begin to believe that life is simply a daily series of gruesome murders.

"There's some of that," Dan Rather agreed, "in fact, there's a great deal of that, both in the newspaper business and in the television business. Violence is one of those things that makes news. What *is* news? It's what people are interested in; it's what people need to know. One of the things that interests people is the unusual. I'll give you an example. This kind of thing happens a lot at local stations. When I worked at the television station in Houston, KHOU-TV, we were number three in the ratings. I had the best police reporter in town, Bob Wolf. He'd come in, put his feet up on the desk, light a cigarette and say, 'What we need, Dan, is more Fuzz and Was'; 'Fuzz' being police, 'Was' being dead bodies. That was his vernacular. If you're going to get from number three in the ratings to number one, you simply must have Fuzz and Was.

"The fact is, we did increase our police reporting on the evening news and the fact is our rating did go up. Now, I can't sit here and tell you that that situation doesn't go on day in and day out at a lot of television stations around the country, because it does. But the high journalistic standards that apply in most television newsrooms are those that are applied at local newspapers. Perhaps even more in television than in newspapers. And for one reason: television is more profitable. That may strike some people as a strange thing to say—the profit is what makes stations go for the ratings with their news. But television is *so* profitable on the entertainment side, a really good station manager can say, Listen, I want to make money on news, but first of all I want a good news product. He's making money on the entertainment side, so he can afford to pay what it costs for a good newsroom."

One of my chief objections to local news broadcasts is that often reporters deliver a story in a tone or point of view that indicates their *own* opinion of the subject; this is not something I am interested in. I tune in the news to find out what's happening, *not* what a reporter thinks of the event. Dan Rather has always impressed me as the perfect example of the broadcast reporter who does not editorialize; he is cool, controlled and saves his opinions for dinner parties.

A few years ago I watched with shock and dismay when a local Los Angeles station hired an anchorman from another station, changed his clothes, his face, his on-air personality, revised the look of the show to fit his new image and then watched his rating rise. The station promoted the fact that he was being paid an enormous salary and was given a Rolls-Royce on signing his new contract. They wrote "opinion" comments for him and cultivated an image of him that was more showbiz than news. And he took the station to the top of the ratings. I wondered aloud to Dan Rather if this was the long-range trend of news in our country.

"It's certainly true that some local stations choose to go that route," he said. "I don't think that, long range, it succeeds. There are certainly some stations that give entertainment with the news and succeed in the short run. I'm a believer, though, in news, hard news. In the long run, when people tune in for the news, they want to know what is going on in the world. What Walter Cronkite has to sell is believability. If your local newsman is not believed, he isn't going to last. Driving a Rolls-Royce won't do it; having the biggest contract in the market won't do it; changing your hairstyle or tie won't do it. What *does* do it is people tuning in night after night, saying, 'That guy is trying to be honest and fair in telling me what's going on, he's believeble.' That's what sells."

Viewers often questioned the credibility of television reporting during the Vietnam war. It was very difficult, at least for me, to get any kind of sense of what was going on over there. The award-winning actor Carroll O'Connor, "Archie Bunker," once blasted the American news media on my show. He claimed that television war correspondents simply did not do their duty in Vietnam; they accepted army press releases as fact and continually misled the American people about the nature of the war; we would have been out of there a lot sooner if the American people had been given a truer picture by the electronic media of the events in Vietnam.

Rather, a veteran of Vietnam reporting, bristled at the sug-

gestion of inaccurate coverage. "Baloney, not true. Every reporter I know in Vietnam was determined to do the best job
he was humanly capable of doing. We made mistakes. I made
a lot of mistakes while I was there, and I spent a year of my
life in Vietnam. But it was not a case of misleading the American people; it *was* a case of a very confused and complex
situation. I was confused before I went to Vietnam, I was
confused while I was there and I was confused when I came
out. It's very easy now to look back and say the press should
have done this and that. But I would argue it was television in
the end that brought the American people around to the brutal
truths of Vietnam; it was people who were willing to put their
lives on the line, willing to go and find out things and say, Look,
as much as I can see, here's what's going on. We didn't do as
good a job as we could have done, we didn't do as good a job
as we should have done, but in the end we did the job."

How far a reporter should go to "get the job done" is a
delicate question, and sometimes can turn into a national issue.
One instance of this involved Dan Rather and former President Richard Nixon. I'm sure many remember their famous
interview when Rather, at one point, seemed to be engaged in
an argument with the President of the United States. The
White House was furious with CBS because of the incident.
I asked Dan if he was reprimanded by his superiors.

"No. However, plenty of words were said to me about it. The
first requisite for excellent reporting is a publisher with guts;
you've got to have a publisher who will stick with you. The
most important thing that happened was that CBS News, so
far as I know, never buckled under. They got a lot of pressure;
they shielded me from a great deal of that pressure, but a lot
of it got to me. Several times, John Ehrlichman went to New
York and suggested to my boss, Richard Salant, that I be given
a 'vacation.' Mr. Ehrlichman always said that jokingly. I can

be forgiven, however, if I fail to see the humor. But CBS News never buckles to that kind of pressure.

"Although it is widely believed what I'm going to say may not be true, I will say to you I had nothing personal against Richard Nixon. I abhorred many of the things he did to my country. But as a person I never knew him. I can think of several occasions, one in particular, where I felt a great deal of compassion for Richard Nixon. One of those occasions was in 1972 when I did a one-hour live interview with him in the Oval Office. By the way, before that interview they lowered the temperature to thirty-seven degrees in hopes that when the lights came on they could keep President Nixon from perspiring until well into the broadcast. This maneuver succeeded, but it made the Oval Office into a deep-freeze.

"After the broadcast, I saw that Richard Nixon was alone. Bob Haldeman was not around. It was one of the few times I ever saw Richard Nixon when Haldeman was not close by. This time, he had the Secret Service, but no one else. He stayed and talked with me for twenty-five minutes after the broadcast and was marvelous. He told stories, he spun a yarn. When was the last time anybody had heard Mr. Nixon spin a yarn? When he walked out of the Oval Office, he went through the doorway —on the floor are the cleat marks Eisenhower left when he used to go out to play golf. Mr. Nixon walked out into the night by himself; over his right shoulder was the Washington Monument, beyond that the dimly lit Jefferson Memorial. Richard Nixon was whistling.

"As I watched him walk to the residence-side of the White House, I thought to myself that if we could have had a tape of those last few moments, Richard Nixon might be understood a great deal better; it was one of the few times I saw him in that light. Most of the time he put up, or had put up, a wall around him, because I think he was a deeply wounded person;

somewhere deep in his psyche he was wounded, and he carried a lot of scar tissue with him. I think if you are going to try to understand Nixon, you have to understand that very important point about him."

I was curious to hear Dan's assessment of President Lyndon Johnson, because I had heard curious stories about him from a friend in the White House press corps. For instance, on an Air Force One flight from the Capital to Texas, Johnson asked a military steward to bring him a Fresca. The boy had forgotten to load in Fresca, and when this was reported to the President, Johnson called the boy over and verbally scorched him, going so far as to tell the boy he just might end up in Vietnam for his omission. So, of course, for the return trip, the soldier loaded in cases of Fresca, a fact the President was well aware of. Once the plane took off, Johnson summoned the boy and ordered a different brand of soft drink. My press corps friend also told me that the President would sometimes call him late at night and ask him to come immediately to the White House to give an opinion of a documentary that had just been completed about himself. My friend reported that Johnson derived enormous pleasure out of watching these self-serving documentaries. I asked Dan Rather if he thought these stories had any basis in fact.

"Not only possible," Dan said, "but they happened. He was like that. But he was also capable of tremendous compassion for people around him. He was a great paradox. I know of cases where he was extremely sympathetic to low-level workers in the White House. When people got sick he would send flowers and scribble off a note to them. Lyndon Johnson may have been the best President of our time in addressing himself to human problems. So there was that side of him.

"But he did have an enormous ego. It is quite true, for example, that with Lyndon Johnson there was a time during which no camera was ever allowed to shoot him past a certain angle of his face. He had seen pictures of himself and said, Listen, I don't want any more pictures of my big ears. He told his press people that if a cameraman wanted to take his picture, to make sure that it was from the front.

"There are many stories of Johnson scorching reporters for certain stories, and also, as you say, people around him. I remember a makeup man who once got it. Most Presidents, like most reporters on television, use makeup but, believe me, Presidents don't like to talk about it. Before going on television, Lyndon Johnson would always ask Mrs. Johnson, 'How do you think I look, Bird? How do I look?' Sometimes she would tell him the truth, as wives will do. On one particular occasion, shortly after Johnson became President, he asked Mrs. Johnson, 'How do I look, Bird?' And she said in effect, You look godawful, Lyndon, and you'd better get a new makeup person. So Lyndon Johnson, as he liked to say, President of the United States, leader of the free world and half the universe, ordered the makeup person to appear in the Oval Office. And he said to that individual, (I'll clean up the language), 'Are you *trying* to make me look bad?' You can imagine what the poor makeup person was thinking, standing in the Oval Office in front of the President of the United States.

"In any case, he was a man who had the capacity to dominate any landscape he operated in or occupied. He would walk into a room and, not unlike a coyote, sniff out the allegiances of everybody in that room, and then address himself to what he thought were everybody's likes and dislikes. I think this, among other things, led him to keep some of the John Kennedy advisors, such as MacNamara, Rusk and Rostow. I think in his heart he wanted to get rid of these people, but when he came into office he didn't. He followed their advice on the war, and got caught up in the war himself, which was a great tragedy for him. Because then the Vietnam war became the bottom line of the Johnson Presidency."

And now Dan Rather is off the White House beat and sits in that powerful chair from which we hear the news of the nation and the world. But his promotion to that position bodes well for all of us, because he is one of the best reporters, I believe, ever to knock out a story. Long may he run.

WRITERS

*

SUSAN MARGOLIS—Author of a book about fame:
"I think if you're not careful, you can turn into your image,
especially somebody whose image is something that people care
about. An image is invisible; you can never touch it."

*

WILL AND ARIEL DURANT
Connoisseurs of the Past

BEING AN ENTERTAINER, I've always had immediate feedback to my work. As a kid when I produced backyard shows I had to ham it up pretty good to keep the attention of the other kids; I started learning early how to change an act in mid-stride to win a crowd's wavering attention. I spent several years doing one-nighters with Freddy Martin and His Orchestra, learning from each mistake how to better project myself as a singer. The entertainer's ability to draw on the responses of audiences, directors, conductors and producers gives him constant useful information.

In 1963, when I began my talk show, I started to meet another kind of entertainer, a breed whose product is more important than presence or personality. I'm speaking about writers.

Up until 1963 the writers I'd known were mostly television comedy writers. In fact, the three writers for my first talk show were Dick Cavett, Pat McCormick and David Lloyd. Dick went on to become a stand-up comic and then, of course, a popular television host. David Lloyd gained the respect of the industry for his brilliant work on "The Mary Tyler Moore Show." And Pat continues to be a writer of comedy, an actor and all-around lunatic. It was Pat McCormick who invited me to a party at his home to introduce his first child to his friends. We all arrived and looked around for the baby, who was nowhere in sight. When all the guests were finally assembled, Pat walked into the living room carrying a silver-domed platter, the kind you see in a fancy restaurant; he lifted the lid and there, surrounded by potatoes, carrots and parsley, was his unclad offspring, looking bewildered by the entire experience.

But the kind of writers I started to meet on my talk show were new to me. They were men and women who spent their days in isolation, confronting their muse and challenging their intellect, hoping to produce in a year's time, or two years or ten years, a book that would be read and remembered. With writers begin the ideas which are taught and debated in schools, watched in movies and on Broadway stages. Theatrical entertainers by their performances can elicit the emotions within us; writers give us entirely new emotions. Because I'm used to the instant feedback of the stage and television, I had developed a deep curiosity and respect for these people who labor privately, relying on their instincts to guide their work.

After he completed *Roots* Alex Haley described an incident that for me pinpoints a writer's confrontation with his work. It was during a period of his research when the work wasn't going well. He was on a freighter, returning from Africa, contemplating the horrendous methods used to transport the slaves to America. One night he stood on the stern of the boat in a deep depression. Haley was out of money, the book seemed too big for him ever to complete; his life felt hopeless. He thought how easy it would be to step off the boat into the dark waters below and put an end to his misery. But before he could take the final step, a wave of feeling overcame him; the ghosts of his ancestors surrounded him and held him in place; he *had* to finish the book because the story of his people *had* to be told.

Truman Capote once spoke with me about the writing of *In Cold Blood*, the story of two young killers which became an international bestseller. Capote took on the project because he wanted to experiment with writing nonfiction in the form of a novel. But during the research, which continued for seven years, he felt his own life enveloped by the lives of the murderers. Every waking moment, every dream, every conversation he had during those seven years was aimed at coming to an understanding of the events that made two young men capable of brutally murdering an entire family. Late in 1982 Truman talked about a book he'd been writing in stages for twenty-five years, and *its* completion was now consuming his life; the book carries the slightly ironic title of *Answered Prayers*.

*

JOHN HUSTON:
"Humphrey Bogart wasn't tough, and he wasn't all that strong. I remember one time when he and Truman Capote were arm-wrestling, and it developed into a fight. Truman is a rough little cat, and he had Bogie's shoulders pinned to the floor."

*

I see nobility in the writer's quest to make our times and lives a bit more comprehensible. Two writers who come to mind in this regard are Will and Ariel Durant, authors of the famous series of books collectively known as *The Story of Civilization*. I met them when Will was ninety-two years old and Ariel was a mere eighty.

I was sitting in my office one afternoon discussing upcoming shows, and one of our bookers mentioned that the Durants had expressed an interest in appearing with me. I was quite surprised, knowing they were serious historians and not given to making television appearances. But it turned out that they had described their day to a publicist: breakfast together, research and writing all day, dinner together, watch "The Merv Griffin Show," and then retire for the evening. The publicist asked them if they'd like to be interviewed by me and they asked unbelievingly, "Merv would really want to talk to *us*"? When I heard that I had a good laugh, and the offer was made immediately. A tape date was set, and we invited James Michener and Irving Stone to join the Durants on the panel.

We dispatched one of our writers to preinterview Will and Ariel Durant; he came back to the office looking confused. I asked him how the session had gone.

"All right, I *guess.*"

"What do you mean?"

"Well, I didn't get much of an interview out of them."

"Why the hell not?" I said.

"Because they had a whole list of questions they wanted to ask *me.*"

"About what?"

"The show. They watch it every night, and they had about a hundred questions. They wanted to know if you *really* like all the guests on the show, or if you actually hate a few of them. They wanted to know who your favorite guests were, how you prepare for interviews, who your favorite writers were, and . . ." He stopped and looked out of my office window, shaking his head. "They wanted to know what Charo is like offstage."

I laughed and said, "That's great, but when we do the interview I hope they feel like talking about *their* work."

"Don't worry about that. They let me ask them the questions for five minutes as I was leaving, and they talk about Aristotle and Thomas Aquinas like somebody talking about their neighbors."

We decided to do this show of writers without a studio audience. Certain writers, like Norman Mailer and the wickedly brilliant Gore Vidal, are masters of the media and are as comfortable in front of an audience as they are with their typewriters. But the Durants were used to spending their days quietly reading, thinking and writing; we thought the pressure of a studio audience might make them self-conscious. We guessed wrong.

The first thing Ariel Durant said to me as she walked to the stage with Will was, "Where the heck is your audience? Will stayed up late last night thinking up some jokes for them."

When they sat down, they immediately held hands so I thought it appropriate to ask them about their sixty-five-year collaboration as husband-and-wife writers.

"It comes from mutual tolerance, patience," Will answered, "and the remembrance that there are always at least two sides to everything."

"That's quite prosaic," Ariel said, waving a hand at her husband, "but I imagine quarreling is part of our romance. Just imagine what the world would be like if nobody quarreled and nobody had different degrees of hatred or dislike, if everybody was just pleasantly tolerant. What a tremendously uninteresting world it would be. Our quarrels are as interesting and necessary as the making up."

"You don't throw vases at him, do you, Ariel?"

"I don't see why I shouldn't," she answered with a shrug.

After studying the history of civilization for the past seventy years, did they think we will ever reach a point where we'll have complete tolerance in our society, or is that just a dream?

"You wouldn't *want* it," Ariel insisted. "What would complete tolerance mean? It would be a lack of individuality, a lack of great and strong differences, passions and power. So thanks for our *in*tolerance; to some extent, it's good."

"I thought the message of the 1960s," I said to them, "was that America needed to head into a great age of brotherly love. Young people wanted to be the generation of 'love.'"

"I hope not," Ariel replied crisply. "That would be terrible. We'd all become like prim puritans going around preaching brotherly love. I think hatred is very important in life. Hatred of what you dislike. Hatred of what you think is injurious.

Hatred of differences you wish didn't exist. Hatred is just as important as love."

Will smiled patiently and commented, "Merv, she loves the idea of being terrible, but she can't succeed." He turned to his wife and said, "Let me tell Merv about some of your escapades. I used to go to Columbia University and do a lot of research in biology and forget about Ariel all day long, and she grew tired of that. So one day I came back and there was nobody home. We lived on Staten Island then. It turned out that she had got the brilliant idea of finding out how justice operates in the United States.

"She went to Manhattan, and I forget what she did to provoke it, but a policeman got hold of her. She was happy about that and told the policeman to arrest her. She went before a judge, who asked her what was the nature of her crime. 'I just wanted to see how you people practice justice,' she told him.

"So the judge decided she was crazy and told her, 'We have a place in Bellevue Hospital that is just the thing you'd enjoy.' They took her to the hospital and put her in the insane asylum. A certain Dr. Gregory came by, looked at her and decided at once that she was ninety-five percent crazy. She had a devil of a time getting out of Bellevue because she couldn't make them believe she had started this as an enterprise in sociology. Finally she persuaded Dr. Gregory to let her write to me. Now, he didn't believe she *had* a husband; however, to humor her, he mailed the letter. Naturally, I'd been hunting all over the world, never thinking to look in an insane asylum. I found her and she said, 'Take me home, Will, I found out all I want to know.' "

Ariel smiled at the memory and added: "Before discharging me, the doctor told me to write down my ideas about the incident. The first thing I did was to write down that Dr. Gregory was crazy. He decided, after reading it, that I should be kept there. Will admitted to the doctor that I *was* crazy, but that he would look out for me. So I had it out with him later."

At that point we broke for a commercial, and my writer's warning came true. The Durants leaned over and said to me, "Now tell us about yourself and your show," and they peppered me with questions for the next few minutes. I found their curiosity a lesson in longevity. I'm sure all of us know elderly people who have reached a point in life where they don't *want* to hear about anything new. But the Durants were insatiably curious about my role as host of the show, about the technical aspects of the cameras and about the guests who get the biggest response from audiences. This was a new experience for them and they wanted to make the most of it.

Ariel Durant seemed to lead a life feminists of the sixties and seventies strived for: that rare combination of fulfilling a noteworthy career *and* having a successful marriage. I asked if those two turbulent decades would produce great women of history. To my surprise, she shook her head and suggested that history's greatest women lived four hundred years ago.

"They were the great women of the salon," Ariel explained. "In France especially, there was a tradition that women were the only ones who were refined; the men were always out in the field, they were warriors and uncouth. The manners of a nation were the responsibility of the women, particularly in sixteenth-century France, when the women ran great salons. They were not only educated but taught manners to the courtiers and the generals. It was these women who kept education and refinement going. Men returned from the wars with their crude mannerisms, so it was up to the women of that time to educate not only the children but also the men. Men were a crude element before the advent of women's consciousness;

women exemplified the manners and morals that we judge countries by. The aristocracy of Italy were the first of the educated in Europe; they had great gentility in manners. From there it spread to France, and later to the more masculine countries like England and Scotland. Therefore, a great deal of what we are today in terms of refinement, manners and morals is due to the women of the thirteenth, fourteenth and fifteenth centuries. They were not content that men had saved civilizations through war. *They* were the ones carrying on education." Today's young women who say they are attempting to "humanize" men, Ariel suggested, are only following a tradition.

Our conversation gradually led to the state of the world today. I wondered if the chaos we confront each morning when we open a newspaper was any different from the turmoil at other points of man's history. What were the signs of true decay in a civilization?

Will answered: "When the moral code loses its force on human beings, largely through the decline of religious beliefs that had strengthened them. We know historically that all civilizations eventually decline. We can see Greece declining, for example, in 200 B.C. We can see Rome decline in A.D. 100. I am afraid we are at present in danger of being at the same stage, where the religious basis of our moral code has been weakened, and the code itself is no longer strong enough to maintain social order.

*

TIMOTHY LEARY—Former Harvard professor, famous for his advocacy of LSD:
"I had come to the sorry conclusion that psychology wasn't doing much to solve the emotional and mental problems of the human race, especially the American people. So I went to Mexico, and a friend of mine, an anthropologist, told me about

a method which had been used by the Indians in Mexico, administered by the medicine man before the white man came. They used mushrooms, 'sacred mushrooms.' One sunny Saturday afternoon he brought over a bag of the mushrooms and I ate seven of them. And I learned more about psychology, about the human mind and the human situation in the five hours after eating the mushrooms than I had learned in a career of research in psychology and treating people as a psychotherapist.

"It is true that LSD provides an ecstatic experience. The pleasure you get from LSD is from being tuned in, turned on to your own nervous system, turned on to your own body; you are turned on to an incredible wisdom which lies inside every cell."

*

"Police are not enough. The old belief in religion was as if God *and* a policeman were on every corner; He isn't there anymore. Religious beliefs are a vital factor in every civilization, because the State itself is not strong enough to maintain social order. Without religion, we probably wouldn't have *had* a civilization. It was the use of supernatural beliefs to control the individualistic instincts of the human being that made civilization possible. When that belief dies, or is seriously weakened, civilization itself runs into an age of permissiveness and moral chaos, such as we are enjoying today. There have been periods like that in other civilizations, but they were cured by their own excess. Then it went to another extreme; the pagan period is usually followed by a puritan reaction. Then another pagan period comes as a reaction to the puritan period. Civilizations constantly go to excess, and then destroy themselves."

After the interview, which contained plenty of intrafamily disagreement, Will said to Ariel, "How have you managed to *stand* me all these years?"

She answered, "Very easily. I'm still in love with you. If I stopped loving you I don't want to live."

Ariel Durant became ill and died last year. Three weeks after her death, Will followed.

JAMES JONES
War and Peace in Paris

I FIRST VISITED Paris in 1963, for only a couple of chilly, bleak days that didn't endear the city to me. In 1965 I returned to France, this time with a film crew, to do interviews for my newly revived talk show. Prior to our arrival in Paris, my staff contacted some of the more famous expatriate Americans residing in the city. One of them was the author of *From Here to Eternity*, James Jones. Not only did he consent to do an interview, he wanted to throw me a party, just to make sure I got the trip off to a proper start. Another American author of considerable literary reputation, Irwin Shaw, was also staying in Paris and joined Jones in toasting my welcome to the City of Light.

If the welcome had been limited to just one toast, I might have gotten by without a headache the next day. "In America somehow there is a terrible affinity between writers and booze," Irwin Shaw told me later, "just to get a vacation from your head." I made the mistake of trying to keep up, drink for drink, with Jones and Shaw, and the combination of booze and jet lag nearly finished me off.

"I have the unfortunate ability to drink a great deal and never have a hangover," Irwin said when I reminded him of the party. "I have a doctor in Paris who has seen how much

235

I have drunk through the years. I went to him just recently, because I had a cold, and he said, 'While I have you here, lie down.' He began to feel my liver and his face fell. 'It's so *unjust,*' he said, 'your liver is in perfect condition.' "

The party broke up just as dawn was coming up over Paris, and that gave me only a couple of hours' sleep, because I was due back at 10 A.M. on the Île St. Louis, where the Joneses lived, to do an interview with James.

James Jones arrived promptly at ten, looking ragged but mentally alert. I was ragged, period. We sat on some stone steps facing the Seine, sipping coffee and squinting into the bright sun. I think the *clochards,* Paris's famous bums who live beneath the bridges of the Seine, felt a little sorry for us as they watched from the shade while we filmed our interview.

Gloria and James Jones moved to Paris in 1958, steeped in the tradition of American expatriate writers such as Ernest Hemingway and F. Scott Fitzgerald.

"I'd never been to France," James recalled, "but I had an idea for a book about American jazz musicians and Negroes living in Paris. I came to spend a year, then we stayed. I don't know what it is that made us stay. The city, for one, is beautiful; it's an aesthetic pleasure to walk around the streets of Paris. You can't say that about New York or Hollywood; maybe you could say it about San Francisco. But just to your eyeball alone, it's a pleasure to walk around here. And then there's the great tradition of artists and painters and writers who have all lived here."

I asked him how America looked after eight years away from it. "Living abroad actually makes me less critical of America," he said. "It calls up a nostalgia in me that cuts down my sense of criticism. I would be much more critical of America living there."

Both Jones and his friend Irwin Shaw have enjoyed the unusual combination of critical acceptance and commercial popularity. At this point in Jones's life he was questioning the benefits of the success he had so doggedly pursued.

"Success makes you believe in yourself, and that can be very bad. What I think happens is if you are going to be a writer, you're going to have such an inordinate vanity to begin with that you say to yourself, 'Screw the world, I can do this, I *will* do this,' and you do it. But then you begin to have a lot of sychophants and people hanging around who tell you, 'You're the greatest writer, the best.' And you begin to believe that you are. Then the same vanity that was your aide and your protector when you were young and broke and scared becomes a poisonous enemy. I wrote *From Here to Eternity* while living in a house trailer, moving through Colorado, Arizona, New Mexico, Montana. I lived that way four years, pulling this thing from trailer park to trailer park. I would write in the mornings, then farm and hunt in the afternoons. Material success changes that way of life. It can be dangerous when that happens."

Didn't living in Paris on the Île St. Louis, with a view of Notre Dame and a stone's throw away from the world-famous restaurant La Tour D'Argent, have to be a more favorable atmosphere for writing than a trailer?

"No," he said, shaking his head and looking at the murky water of the Seine. "Everything is terrible for writing. I need a blank wall and a typewriter. If I have a window or a good view I never work, I'll sit and look at the view. If there's something hanging on the wall, a painting, I'll look at that."

Like the Durants, Orson Welles and many other creative giants I've encountered, James Jones felt the pressure of many projects to complete and so little time to attend to them all. He had five or six future books in mind, one in particular. "I'd like to write a combat novel about the Civil War as it *really* was, not as it was written about by the romantic novelists of that period. In the first place, sex was out in those books, they couldn't talk freely about it, yet in reality there was an awful lot of sex going on around the countryside during the war. Secondly, amputations were enormous. If you got hit with a minié ball in your arm or leg, you lost the arm or leg. Today, we've got great medicine to save an arm that's hit. That makes interesting material because men went into combat *knowing* that if they got hit in the gut they were dead. This is interesting stuff for a writer to tackle."

Jones had spent much time fighting, contemplating it and writing about it; it was the driving force behind his greatest writing. But he was older now, a father, and I wondered what he would tell his son about war.

"I would tell him to stay out of any war he could stay out of, but that if he did, he'd probably regret it later. It's a very ambivalent position, and I don't know fully how to explain it to anybody. All of us old men who were in it are now glad we were and wouldn't have missed the experience for the world. But we have a tendency to forget the painful parts and remember the good.

"As long as one man is willing to fight another man for an ideal, no matter how profound and brilliant, you have a race that is going to wage war on each other. There are different moral codes working in war. I grew up taught to fight fair, don't kick in the crotch, don't kick a guy in the head when he's on the ground; be honest, truthful and brave, all the Boy Scout virtues. Those don't work anymore, not in war. Irwin Shaw told me a story about a Ranger sergeant at Anzio who got eleven new replacements in his outfit one day. A few days later the outfit got the order to go out and make a 'feeling attack' outside their own minefields. They all knew it was a bust; there was no way they could do anything, it was sewed up tight as a drum. So this platoon sergeant sent the eleven young greenhorns out first. And, of course, they were all killed. But he didn't lose any of his old men. He said, 'I couldn't send my buddies out into that deathtrap. We didn't know these kids, they were green-horns. We'd been fighting together in Africa, Sicily, Salerno and Anzio. I'm not about to send my pals out there. So I sent the kids. But how do I explain that to my wife or my mother? They don't understand.'

"What I'm getting at is that war is a different morality entirely. It's a much crueler morality. It's all based on the family, which is the squad, the platoon, the company, the battalion. In war they're the only friends you've got and you can't trust them most of the time. But that's the morality you live with in war."

War seemed a difficult subject to contemplate on a sunny spring morning in Paris, but only because I was not James Jones. He excused himself. It was time to return home to write.

JERZY KOSINSKI
Taking Chances

SEVERAL YEARS AGO I flew aboard the Concorde from New York to Paris, where I was to meet my son for a week's vacation. My secretary had arranged a limousine to pick me up at the airport and deliver me in town. Our flight arrived quite late at night and the airport wasn't crowded. Even so, I couldn't find my driver. After half an hour of searching, I stood in front of the terminal, perturbed. A tall, trim man with dark curly hair and notably intense eyes approached me, accompanied by a woman. I remembered him from the flight. "I can't help but recognize you," the man said, "I watch your show frequently and enjoy it very much."

He had an accent that I couldn't place, so when he introduced himself I wasn't able to clearly make out his name . . . Jerry something. We chatted a few minutes and he told me he was in Europe for the polo matches, his hobby.

"Well," Jerry said, "it's been a pleasure talking to you and I'd love to be on your show sometime back in New York."

That's a strange thing for someone to say, I thought to myself; he was a very nice guy, but why would I put him on my show?

When I returned to the States I mentioned the incident to one of my writers; I thought he could write a funny monologue about it for me. Wasn't that an odd thing for someone to say? "And he was serious, he wanted to be on the show," I said.

"He was a polo player," my writer said.

"Yes, that was just his hobby though. His name was Jerry Cuzzins, or something like that. He talked so fast I could hardly understand him."

"Was he tall and thin?"

"Yes, how did you know that?"

"Was there a woman with him named Kiki?"

"As a matter of fact, yes. That was her name, Kiki."

"Then," the writer said, "you just met Jerzy Kosinski."

"You mean the author of *Being There*"?

"That's the guy."

"He must think I'm nuts because when he said he'd like to be on my show I think I looked a little shocked." I knew his novel *Being There* quite well, and had certainly heard of *The Painted Bird* and *Steps*. It was all a little embarrassing, but then it was James Michener who had once told me that the great thing about being a successful writer is people know your name, but not your face; you get a good room in a hotel, but no one bothers you in public.

Shortly after my return to Los Angeles, I received a brief note from Kosinski; we called him immediately and invited him to do the show on our upcoming trip to New York. His own story is more engrossing than almost anyone else's novels. He survived the Holocaust by living as a vagabond in Poland, and finally bluffed his way into America, where he worked as a parking attendant while studying English at night. Even though he is now writing in a second language, he has emerged as a major literary stylist, and another shining example of an American dream come to life. He is certainly an advocate of the possibilities presented in this country to become whatever we have the courage to become.

"We don't take enough chances with our own lives," he told

me; "we behave as if we were immortals. We don't change often enough. We behave as though we were defined by totalitarian systems, while in fact we are absolutely free to remodel ourselves, to find new experiences, perhaps to find a new self, and that's the only freedom there is. This is the only country that allows you to do it, that allows you not to be bound by your vital existence.

That's the core of the Protestant message, that you don't have to be bound. This is the great thing about this country, the main ethnic it demands of you—that you *cannot* remain passive, because then you are at the mercy of your vital existence and you are no longer a spiritual being. Now to have that kind of climate *and* the political freedom that accompanies it, my God, what else do you want?"

*

LIV ULLMANN—On relationships:
"There's nobody who is one block of harmony. We are all afraid of something, or feel limited in something. We all need somebody to talk to. But maybe instead of going to a psychiatrist it would be good if we talked to each other—not just pitter-patter, but really *talk*. We shouldn't be so afraid, because most people really like this contact; that you show you are vulnerable makes *them* free to be vulnerable, too. And then we don't wear these masks. It's so much easier to be together when we drop the masks."

*

JAMES MICHENER
Making Curiosity Pay

A WRITER WHOSE life embodies the ability to change, as Kosin-ski describes it, is James A. Michener. He was an orphan, lived a rough-and-tumble adolescence, moved through a variety of jobs and did not write his first book until he was forty years old. That first book, *Tales of the South Pacific,* won him critical recognition and financial rewards, but the early success only spurred him on. He has since given us such entertaining and informative works as *Hawaii, The Source* and *Centennial.* His own story is so encouraging that I hope he writes it one day.

"I believe I'm the only one living now who started writing at forty and stayed with it," he told me when we met for the first time in the early seventies. "A lot of people at forty or fifty write a single book; I think everybody can write one book, every human life has a dramatic form that can be externalized for the benefit of other people. But to come back two or three times, even four or five, requires a professional capacity, and most of us don't have that. I started very late, and was lucky to get off the ground.

"I was an orphan. I grew up in a little town in Pennsylvania. I have no clear idea who my parents were; I believe I was a foundling. I was moved into a marvelous family consisting of three sisters who took care of abandoned children. So I grew

245

up in an absolutely fascinating setting, where children would move in every five or six months, and I'd constantly have new brothers and sisters. This remarkable woman, the oldest of the three sisters, who I'm not even sure had gone through high school, would become attached to some of the kids. She lived an absolutely horrible life of abject poverty, made a living by taking in laundry and sweatshop sewing of buttons. She held on to some of us and put two of us through college, and three others through high school. I remember being at home on Christmas when I was about thirty-eight, and the whole day, dawn to dusk, consisted of people coming to our house with presents for these three women; they had done so much good in their society.

"Every night they would read to us after supper. I heard Dickens and Thackeray and Cervantes and the rest of the classics. I think a lot of my narrative style comes from that, hearing the great storytellers read to me."

The fascination with stories and the curiosity about life instilled in Jim Michener by these women never left him. His energy for learning is boundless. We called him once about a show we were putting together, involving the darker side of America's sports mania, a subject he had written extensively on in *Sport in America*. We reached him at his temporary home on the Chesapeake Bay, during a bitterly cold and slushy winter. But when Jim heard the issue and the people we hoped to present on our program, he took a few days out of his writing schedule to fight the weather, fly three thousand miles to Los Angeles and appear on the panel. He was seventy years old at the time, but if he was feeling the effects of jet lag, he wasn't showing it. We sent a staff member with the limousine to bring him to the studio, and during the twenty-minute ride from the Beverly Hills Hotel to our facility James Michener drained our writer of every possible bit of information about our taping.

When he arrived in our Green Room he was introduced to

the president of my company, Murray Schwartz. Several months earlier Murray had been one of the hostages held in Uganda just before the Israeli rescue mission. This was mentioned to Jim Michener, and he used the few minutes left before taping to ask Murray several questions about the experience—he never knew when the information might come in handy for a book. As always, his comments during the taping were insightful and entertaining. He then went directly to the airport; on the way out the door he said he was anxious to get back to the typewriter and complete his Chesapeake novel, because he was already in the planning stages of a new novel about South Africa.

On his next visit to California—a way station for his ultimate destination, Hawaii, where he was going to host several public television specials based on his work—I had the opportunity to ask him about his ceaseless energy.

"I think nobody writes a book like the ones I have written without an enormous internal drive," he said, "which can be equated with vanity or a challenge to the world. I have often thought that if one were completely normal psychologically, he wouldn't *have* to write. I have a terrible inner drive that some men have, and it stems from their childhood experience. I've always been very rebellious. I ran away from home several times. I was thrown out of every school I ever attended. I was a fighter. I think I lived a little more harshly than I needed to. But I think that if I had not fought so harshly as an adolescent, I never would have developed the commitment that I've had. One thing the books I've written testify to is that when I *did* get started, I had a heck of a head of steam; I think that comes from an early commitment that I wasn't ever going to live in the poorhouse. But from my experience, I am never going to turn my back against the guy at the bottom of the heap. I cannot afford to ignore or degrade anybody because I really don't know who I am. I may be Jewish, I might be Oriental,

I might be part Negro. So I embrace all.

"What drives me, too, is a great inner compulsion to communicate. I really have sometimes thought that the only thing I can do in this world, the only thing I'm confident about, is to communicate. Writing is *very* hard for me. But I'm quite confident that if I took the time to describe a chair in about three paragraphs I could make you read it. I recall a story told by the great writer Dumas. A young man approached him and said, 'Monsieur Dumas, I have read your novels *The Musketeers*, and I know how you do what you do. And *I* have the greatest plot there ever was.'

"Dumas says to him, 'Does it have suspense?'

" 'Yes, absolutely.'

" 'Do you have any characters?'

" 'I have characters, a marvelous girl and heroic man.'

" 'Do you have a good setting?'

" 'Yes, France, at the age of its glory.'

"And Dumas said, 'Then you are a very lucky man. Now all you need is two hundred and fifty thousand words!'

"It is the moving of ideas into words that is the trick to the whole thing," Michener concluded.

That is a fundamental phrase, "moving ideas into words." We've all hatched brilliant schemes and plots at cocktail parties or while lying in a hammock, but it is the rare person who *does* anything about it. For Michener the crucial moment came during the war.

"I was on a small island south of Guadalcanal. I remember listening to the fellows bitch about it dreadfully. And it suddenly occurred to me that here were the best young men America had ever produced, and it couldn't be a negative experience; it *had* to be positive, because positive people were there. I knew that afternoon that when the years had passed, they would want to read about this experience and compare their experiences with those of other guys. I wrote from this very modest intention. I wanted to get on record something the fellows could come back to in ten, fifteen years.

"I was right about that. Fifteen years later *Tales of the South Pacific* was selling as well as when it was first published. Only because the human experience is always viable, it's always good, and I think one of the most extraordinary things about the last few years is that nobody has written a really fine book about Vietnam. I suppose all the people involved in it were ambivalent, from the generals on down. You don't have terrific impetus to write when you have an ambivalent feeling about something. You have to either be with it or against it. You can't write well otherwise."

Jim Michener has a great love for America. As Jerzy Kosinski pointed out, this is a country where you can change your life, become anything you are big enough to become. In this regard I asked Jim about our future. As part of his extensive traveling (which has continued into his middle seventies) he meets a great cross section of Americans, particularly young people, in whose hands rest the decades to come.

"I have grave doubts about this sometimes," he says, "then soaring hopes. The doubts come from the deterioration of education. Publishers are taking books which we used to use in high school, dressing them up and using them for the sophomore or junior year in college. That is a loss to all of us, especially to the kids. But also to you and me, because where are our successors going to come from? We had a terrible case in Washington not long ago, in which a local college was involved in a fight over four of its students. The argument was should they be given certificates to teach mathematics. The teachers of the four students said they couldn't add fractions, couldn't reduce a fraction to a decimal, couldn't solve a simple quadratic equation and you want *them* to go out and teach the *next* generation? The principal of the school said these students were nice guys, they've been here four years, they haven't given us any trouble, they really deserve their degrees. And they *got* their degrees.

"On the other hand, I see a lot of young people, and the good ones are better than I was at their age; they're sharper, brighter and quicker. There is a lot of talent. But I think talent in this world is very ordinary, very common. There's plenty of it. However, disciplined talent is very, very rare."

*

JAMES A. MICHENER:
"One of the most profound experiences of my life came in the period from 1934 to 1940, when everybody said America had gone soft, especially the young people. Everybody told me that American youth was finished. And then what happens? 1941. You take those same kids, and throw them in Guadalcanal, which must be the worst battlefield anybody ever fought on. Our kids were fighting the Japanese, a very able, tremendous enemy. And our young men performed as heroically as any young men in history. I would think that same capability still resides within us. What we have to do is divert that energy into more creative areas, but I would not think that if a real test came our young people would crumple. I think there would be a tremendous resilience there."

*

I'm sure there are many motivations behind those writers who combine talent with the discipline necessary to write, and rewrite books. But a common clue might be found in the words of Irving Stone. He has spent a lifetime studying greatness, having written novelized biographies of such men as Michelangelo, Vincent Van Gogh, Sigmund Freud and Charles Darwin. I asked Irving once if he'd found a thread that runs through the life of all these exceptional people. He told me:

"I write about people who sometime in their life . . . have a vision or dream of something that should be accomplished . . . and they go to work. They are beaten over the head, knocked down, vilified and for years they get nowhere. But every time they're knocked down they stand up. You cannot destroy these people. And at the end of their lives they've accomplished some modest part of what they set out to do."

This, I believe, applies to the lives of many of our best writers. I salute the ones I know, and also the ones I wish yet to know.

Suddenly there is a loud noise!
Hiccup and his friends rush
toward the noise.
When they arrive, they are shocked.

The dragons broke into
the village storehouse.
They ate all the food
that the Vikings were storing
for the freeze!

Even Toothless is guilty.

Soon Mildew and the other Vikings
arrive.
They are very angry.
"You need to send these
dragons away!" Mildew shouts.

"You're right, Mildew,"
Chief Stoick says.
"We will cage them tonight, and
Hiccup will send them away
in the morning."

At dinner Hiccup and his friends
are very sad.
They don't want to send their
dragons away.
But Hiccup has an idea.

"The dragons are going to do
what they're going to do,"
Hiccup tells his friends.
"It's in their nature.
We just have to learn to use it."

The next day Hiccup and
his friends decide to work with
the dragons—not against them.

The dragons scare fish
into the Vikings' nets and
chase sheep into their pens.

The dragons plant food
instead of stealing it.
They even help Mildew
plant his field!

"Great job, dragons!"
the Vikings cheer.
Chief Stoick is so proud of Hiccup
and his friends, he gives them
their very own dragon training
academy.

Hiccup is excited.

He can't wait to begin.

"Dragons are powerful, amazing creatures," he says.

"And I'm going to learn everything about them."